JOBS AND JUSTICE, HOMES AND HOPE

Jobs and Justice, Homes and Hope

Sir Fred Catherwood

Hodder & Stoughton
LONDON SYDNEY AUCKLAND

Unless otherwise indicated, Scripture quotations are taken from
the HOLY BIBLE, NEW INTERNATIONAL VERSION.
Copyright © 1973, 1978, 1984 by International Bible Society.
Used by permission. All rights reserved.

Christopher Hill, *Intellectual Origins of the English
Revolution*, Oxford University Press, 1965 is quoted by
permission of Oxford University Press.

Copyright © Sir Fred Catherwood, 1997
Foreword copyright © Roy Clements, 1997
First published in Great Britain 1997

The right of Sir Fred Catherwood to be identified as
the Author of the Work has been asserted by him in
accordance with the Copyright, Designs and Patents Act 1988.

1 3 5 7 9 10 8 6 4 2

British Library Cataloguing in Publication Data
A record for this book is available from the British Library

ISBN 0 340 69072 0

Typeset by Hewer Text Composition Services, Edinburgh
Printed and bound in Great Britain by
Cox & Wyman Ltd., Reading, Berkshire

Hodder and Stoughton Ltd
A Division of Hodder Headline PLC
338 Euston Road
London NW1 3BH

To Angharad

CONTENTS

FOREWORD

After a long period of lamentable neglect, the last twenty-five years have witnessed the re-entry of evangelical Christians into the public debate about social issues. One or two significant Christian voices never abandoned that arena in the first place. Fred Catherwood is one of these. He brings to this analysis of the state of Britain at the end of the twentieth century the wisdom gained from a lifetime of involvement in industry, economics and politics. His more recent engagement in the work of the Evangelical Alliance has given him the opportunity to research thoroughly just what life is like these days at the grass-roots of British society. It is not a happy picture. But local churches serving their communities can make a difference. And only if they do will the Christian gospel carry credibility and the public policy recommendations of Christians be heeded.

Jesus's famous story of the Good Samaritan remains a searching indictment of religious piety which can observe need and distress and yet 'pass by on the other side'. This book invites us to face up to the challenge of neighbour-love in our morally and socially damaged contemporary world. It will have achieved its purpose if, like that parable, it pricks our consciences and motivates us to action.

Roy Clements
Cambridge 1996

INTRODUCTION

We ought to be secure and happy, but instead we are moody and introspective. We have had fifty years of peace; the only possible enemy, the Soviet Union, has collapsed and its ideology with it. The threat of the nuclear holocaust has gone. We are three times as rich as we were in the fifties. Our health is better, we live longer, we can travel cheaply all over the world. We are far better educated and entertained. And there should not be a cloud on the horizon. But we are anxious and discontent.

One reason is that the social solidarity, which held us together as a nation in the toughest times, has evaporated. The most obvious sign is that couples find it hard to stay married. Nearly half of marriages now break up and a lot of couples who live together do not trust each other enough to commit themselves to marriage. So every year at least eighty thousand children, who love both their parents, lose one of them because their father and mother cannot stand each other. This touches all levels of society. In the Queen's immediate family all four marriages have collapsed: sister, daughter and both married sons.

The rate of violence against the person, especially by teenagers, has soared. There is a new world of selfishness and hate, with senseless vandalism – a crime which did not even exist until this generation.

The debris of this social collapse is scattered all around. There are still eight times as many unemployed as there were in the fifties and sixties; trades union solidarity is a fading memory; we have sweated labour and work the longest hours in the European

Union. There are beggars on the streets, and some of the new slums and those who live in them would do credit to Dickens' imagination. In every town and city there are boys sleeping rough and an increase in teenage prostitution.

The moral order has collapsed too. Violence, especially by teenage boys, has soared. Most crimes are not dealt with, and if they were there would be no prisons for those convicted, despite an increase in prison accommodation of 50 per cent. There are extensive no-go areas where there is no point in reporting crimes. As people – from unwanted children to confused adults – face personal problems for which they no longer have any spiritual hope or moral guidance, they turn to drugs and the plague of addiction is now endemic.

It is not just the unemployed teenager on a no-hope estate who has turned to thieving. There are too many in the City of London, entrusted with other people's money, who have creamed off the best of the profits for themselves. They extend from the City's jewel in the crown, Lloyds of London, to a once proud city bank, Morgan Grenfell, now bailed out by its new German owners to protect their own reputation.

Riches have not made us generous. Ahead of the 1997 election, neither of the major parties have dared to mention the possibility of higher taxes either to meet urgent social needs or to allow a reduction in interest rates to encourage investment and jobs. All the talk is about cutting public expenditure even further. Schools shut down because the funds for looking after disruptive pupils have run out. Hospital waiting lists get longer again. Those who can least afford it are encouraged to waste their money on the lottery so that government gains an extra source of revenue without raising taxes. No one even mentions the two million people who are still out of work and the idea of full employment seems light years away.

But the two major parties have decided that it is the votes of those who are in work that they need if they are to gain power. The unemployed are outside their political reckoning. Neither proposes any alternative.

This book is about alternatives and how to achieve them.

For it, I have drawn on my experience in industry, in British public service and in politics. I have also, in the last year, consulted industry, the trades union leaders, leading think-tanks and academics on the ways of restoring full employment. The TUC, who have consulted widely themselves, have been especially helpful. On this problem I am especially grateful to Sir Richard O'Brien, who led the *Faith in the City* enquiry and who, until recently, chaired the Church Urban Fund.

My most compelling experiences, however, have been the visits over the last four years, made as President of the Evangelical Alliance, to city missions and church projects where Christians are trying to deal with the dire effects of a moral and economic collapse. Our aims were first to see if locally we could help to build city networks so that churches – and others – knew where to send those in need and could accept some collective responsibility for them; second, to see if nationally we could help pass on hard-won experience to those who were just starting. In thirty visits to twenty-five cities we learnt a great deal about the state of the country.

Our small team from the Evangelical Alliance has travelled the country from Aberdeen to Southampton, from the Foyle to the Thames; and the more visits we made to city churches, missions and projects, the clearer we became as to what has gone wrong. The problem is not just unemployment, it is not just the break up of the family; it is a lethal cocktail of both together, interacting on each other. And out of that cocktail come the other chronic problems: homelessness, debt, crime and drugs. Chapter 2 presents the views on what has gone wrong in the words of those who have the tough job of dealing with the results.

Underneath these symptoms is the collapse of the county's moral order: the standard of values which enables us to live together in peace and without taking each other to law at every turn. That collapse of moral order has undermined the family, which has always been the basic institution in our society – and every other.

Sexual freedom turns out to be the freedom of the man to walk out on his wife and children. In only one in ten cases is it the man who is left holding the baby. So the first section of the book is on the moral order – the absolutely unprecedented collapse of the family – as told in the cold figures and then, in Chapter 2, as told in the words of those who have had to deal with all that and with all the problems which follow from family breakdown: depression, homelessness, debt, crime, prostitution and drugs.

I end the section with the case for the rebuilding of the moral order on a basis which is Christian, but which also respects the not very different views of Muslims, Sikhs and Jews, for all of whom the family is also central.

If lust and sexual promiscuity are destroying the family, unrestrained greed is well on its way to destroying employment. It is greed which keeps taxes low and interest rates high, crippling the industrial recovery which we need to restore full employment. It is greed which is beginning to destroy trust in financial institutions on which the commerce of our trading nation depends. It is the willingness to be bribed with our own money which has destroyed the value of the pound over the last thirty years, and it is the possibility of putting this bribery out of the reach of government which is at the heart of the debate on monetary union.

It is not easy to disentangle the strands which cocoon the real issues in this monetary debate, because as soon as you deal with one argument, powerful vested interests confuse it with another – and billionaire newspaper owners as well as other billionaires are among those interests. I have found that the best way to deal with rhetoric is to see what its effect would be if fully put into practice. The effect of monetarism is to make the rich richer and the poor poorer.

In the second section I spell out the practical ways back to full employment. We have done it before and we can do it again. It just needs another set of priorities and the refusal to be put off by the rhetoric of the rich.

In the third section, we come to the public debate on morality which has, at last, broken through the defensiveness of the intellectual establishment, because the deep damage could no longer be concealed.

Thirty years ago, secular humanism started an experiment in social engineering, which has gone disastrously wrong. It began with the proposition that, in a multifaith society, Christianity could no longer have the last word. So, though the loosening of moral restraint was equally objectionable to Muslims, Sikhs and Jews, the way was open for the new dogmas of secular humanism to take over.

It was one thing to sell the new freedom to do as we liked; it is quite another to restore order without any grass-roots organisation, no written moral code which resonates with people's own perceptions and no case law. They don't have a hope! As disorder increases the electorate will begin to call for order at any price and the price of order will be high. It could well be the arrival in power of an authoritarian party, nationalist and populist, Essex man shoulder to shoulder with Bournemouth woman. Our feeble, imprecise constitution, geared to sharing power between two big establishment parties, could easily be blown apart. Our hard-won freedom is fragile, because those who did not realise that the basis of freedom is self-discipline have pushed blindly beyond those bounds.

We have a lot of talk today about 'national identity', but little about its origins. For over a thousand years, our national identity has grown with the growing influence of the Christian faith. The united English church came before we had a united English kingdom.

Christianity was strong in Saxon times, was compromised under our Norman rulers, surged forward under the Tudors, clashed with the Stuarts, was revived at popular level under Wesley, in society under the Clapham Sect, and again, in 1859, the time of Spurgeon and Shaftesbury, enjoyed a great revival. It weakened in the early twentieth century and since then has strengthened again.

The Christian faith is the base of our law and customs. It was responsible for the scientific method and the Protestant ethic which combined to pull us up by our bootstraps. Its respect for the dignity of the individual gave us democracy and the trades unions, and if it collapses Britain as we know it will collapse too.

The most urgent task is to strengthen our weak constitution – the subject of Chapter 10. We need to change our status from subjects – who receive political power by concessions from on high – to the status of citizens, who empower government for a limited period under stated conditions. Most urgently, we need to see that no nationalist populist party – or any other – can be elected by a minority of the voters as it can now.

Finally, in Chapter 12, there is the issue, now breaking through to the public debate, as to who is responsible for the moral state of the nation: church or state. There is a growing realisation that, though government has a duty to keep to its own moral code, it is in no position to preach to the country. 'Back to basics' was an instant flop. But the present climate of opinion is not going to concede this automatically to the Christian church. The church has to earn its own way back as a moral mentor.

I believe that we can regain that position only by working from the bottom up. The parish, the chapel and the mission are where both our strength and duty lie. If we care for the crying needs of our own neighbours, as is our bounden duty, and show real Christian love, then we earn the right to comment on what has gone wrong and what must be done to put it right. We earn that position parish by parish, ward by ward, city by city and finally in Westminster itself.

THE MORAL ORDER

Chapter One

'NOBODY WANTS ME'

The unloved and unwanted generation

The boy had left his father that morning to go back to his mother who had custody. 'But,' he told his teacher, 'I've just rung Mum and she doesn't want me. Where can I go tonight?' No one wanted him, and from that night on he slept rough with all the other unwanted boys on the stairs of the town-centre car-park. That was in a town with plenty of money and jobs, but mean and hard-hearted people.

Usually it is a row between the teenager and Mum's new man which drives them to the cold concrete of the car-park. Sometimes a friend has a place on a floor, sometimes it is a squat; but one way or the other the country is now littered with abandoned teenagers, the debris of the new morality. It is worse for the girls abused by their stepfather who, when they walk out, are too often picked up by the pimps to become teenage prostitutes.

Not all abandoned mothers find a new man. The council estates are now full of single mothers whose men have walked out and left them to struggle on single-handed. In one estate in Edinburgh five hundred children had to be taken into care in one year. We know from the growing number of cases of child abuse that the state cannot find the trusted and experienced carers to cope with that tidal wave of displaced children. There is a hostel in an old farmhouse near Chester, dedicated to keeping families together and out of care. They say that they can tell at once the young children who have been in care. 'They have a hard mask over their faces and it is tough work to get through to them.'

But the loss of a parent, usually a father, leaves a trauma even for those children still at home. In one estate in Edinburgh, the windows of the junior school opposite the City Mission were all smashed and the caretaker's house was shuttered and left empty after he had been mugged for the third time. In a pleasant estate of small houses with pretty gardens in a Yorkshire mining town the school, the library and the church were all surrounded by twelve-feet high steel posts and each house had either an alarm or a guard dog. A mother brought her four-year-old to a jumble sale and the only response the boy would give to anyone was a bark, since the dog's bark was the only friendly response he knew at home.

We are bringing up a generation which owes nothing to anyone; nothing to family, nothing to neighbours and nothing to the social order. They are the loose cannons of our society and may go off in any direction.

Unemployment and family break up, the lethal cocktail

Chronic unemployment makes it far worse. In many of the big estates in our great cities, anything which can be stolen has been stolen. They are no-go areas for the police and people lock themselves in at nights.

Lack of jobs in many cities removes whatever incentive a teacher might try to give young people to learn a trade. If there is a father, the chances are that he is unemployed too. So there is no role model of a normal working life with its disciplines and its friendships, and the gangs make their own role models instead. They are outside the political process. Even if they have homes and are old enough to register as voters, they do not believe that it is worth their while to vote. No one has yet tried to organise them politically, to make them feel that they really matter – to do for them what Hitler did for his Brownshirts, who took over the streets of Germany from the police, as the IRA did with the young unemployed in Derry's Bogside and in West Belfast.

4

The statistics of the last thirty years show an increase in teenage crimes of violence to a level which is greater than any known since Britain first had an organised police force. Forty years ago, in the mid-fifties statistics of my *Economist* diary, muggings (crimes of violence against the person) were not numerous enough to be recorded. The streets of Britain were safe and there was no vandalism. There were in 1953 only forty-one murders in the whole of Britain. Those were the days of Dorothy Sayers, Agatha Christie, Margery Allingham and Michael Innes who-dun-its, when murders in a peaceful community were deeply shocking and when senior policemen – the fictional Applebys and Alleyns – had all the time in the world to investigate what few murders there were. In this violent age, we need blockbusting thrillers or horror movies to rouse our interest.

Divorce

It is not just the working-class families which are breaking up. Divorce started at the top, where the wealthy found it easier to make their way through the law courts. Divorce at will now allows all families to disintegrate with equal ease. Soon one family in two will have come apart and half the children in Britain will know that one parent at least does not think their company worth the trouble of patching up a quarrel or of giving up a rival love.

It is all very well for our intellectual leaders to write about civilised divorce. The churches, who have the job of trying to reconcile partners and of dealing with the trauma of divorce if they fail, know that it is very seldom civilised. The sense of betrayal in the abandoned partner runs very deep and so does the sense of personal worthlessness. Divorce is a seismic shock when it happens, and the quarrels about children and about payment of alimony go on and on.

The shock to the children is just as great. Teachers know that those children whose parents have different surnames are far more likely to be disturbed and to perform below their ability. Churches, who have to pick up the pieces, know all about the depth of the problems and the years it can take for the children to get back to normal life. A generation ago there were grandparents who could step in, but now the grandparents may well be divorced themselves. Too often one parent or both will spoil the child in an attempt to buy its loyalty. But maybe the worst long-term effect is the removal of the role model of marriage as a mutually supporting partnership, buttressed by mutual love and respect; so that failure in one generation breeds failure in the next. Sexual freedom was intended to promote human happiness, not to promote the misery we see all around us. The sexual revolution has created great inequality and bitter unhappiness.

Three Acts of Parliament undermined the family as society's basic social institution. The new divorce laws were not meant to introduce divorce at will; but that has been their effect. The difficulty of obtaining alimony has given the deserted wife little more security than a deserted mistress. The abolition of censorship in the name of freedom of expression let loose a flood of pornography, whose false promise was sex without the complication of personal love and mutual commitment. The third Act was meant to avoid back-street abortions, but it has led to the deaths each year of a hundred and sixty thousand babies in the womb. The introduction of an effective contraceptive pill, added to the assurance that promiscuity need not lead to unwanted and embarrassing babies, was even more potent in the decoupling of sex from marriage.

There was a fourth Act, which could be justified on the grounds that the law should not be unenforceable. It was the legalisation of homosexual acts in private between consenting adults. It is not possible to tell whether this had a direct effect on the key social role of the family; but it was yet another Act of Parliament which accepted the decoupling of sex from marriage.

The secular society

When Britain became a more secular society, there was no debate on whether we should make this change from the Christian moral order which had, for centuries, been the ultimate point of appeal for social justice and social order. Looking back, we can see that we slid into a secular society without any challenge in parliament vigorous enough to force supporters to make the case for their permissive policy. Since then it has not been the church but secular society which has set the agenda, and which must be held primarily responsible for the sharp deterioration in our moral and social order.

The Christian churches are also to blame. Their leaders did not fight their corner. They trimmed weakly to the current secular mood, chipping off this and that Christian belief which did not fit the mood, until exasperated atheists – failing to find a point of conflict – asked whether there was any backbone at all in this wobbling jelly. I once did a TV programme with a trades union leader and the Archbishop of Canterbury. The Archbishop said that we were all too greedy, but the trades union leader asked why his members should not ask for more money. I chipped in to say that there was no point in the Archbishop saying what people should do unless he also said why. It was his job, and his especially, to give a moral reason for social conduct and his authority rested on the Christian faith. But he refused to base his case on his Christian beliefs, so he came over as a feeble do-gooder who knew nothing about human nature. But at least the Archbishop was willing to appear on TV. Too many of those whose private beliefs have stood firm have opted out of the public debate altogether.

The secular humanists have to read the disastrous social statistics as everyone else does. Their whole interpretation of life is governed by feedback from statistics as firmly as the Christian's is governed by moral law. So let us look at the statistics.

Social Trends, 1996 edition, reports in Chapter 2 that,

- The proportion of dependent children living in one-parent families has tripled since 1972 (19 per cent of children now live just with their mother and 1 per cent with their father).
- Twice as many people lived alone in 1994/5 as lived alone in 1961. It is now a quarter of the whole population.
- The proportion of unmarried women aged between eighteen and forty-nine who were cohabiting in Great Britain almost doubled between 1981 and 1994/5 and is now 23 per cent.

7

- Comparing 1961 with 1993, there were seven times the number of divorces in 1993.
- The number of divorces is now almost equal to the number of first marriages.
- The number of children under five affected by divorce in 1993 was 55,000, almost a quarter higher than ten years before.
- The proportion of live births outside marriage is now 32 per cent.
- The number of legal abortions in 1993 was 19 per cent of all fertilities, nearly 160,000.

This break up of the family so clinically set out in these statistics seems to have a clear knock-on effect on crime. Chapter 9 of *Social Trends* shows that the number of criminal offences has gone up from just under 2 per cent of the population in England and Wales in the 1960s to over 10 per cent in 1994, and that just over 40 per cent of offenders are now under twenty-one. A third of all cases of violence against the person were committed by those under twenty-one.

Is this true freedom?

The humanists argue that, before the liberation of the 1960s, all the unhappiness which today leads to divorce was cooped up in bitterness and resentment between two unhappy people sentenced to live with each other for life.

But can we really believe that half of all the marriages before the 1960s were of people cooped up in bitterness and resentment? It is surely more likely that when marriage really was for life, young people (and their parents) took a lot more trouble to make sure that they really suited each other and that the relationship would pass the test of time. It is also surely true that if divorce was not an option, couples had much more incentive to work out mutually acceptable solutions to their differences. And this argument leaves out of account the damage of divorce to children, the alienation of an unloved and unwanted generation.

Today, when our feelings count for everything, that argument seems to put discipline in place of romance. But discipline is needed in personal relationships. Once there are two instead of one, self-indulgence has to give way. Professions of love are tested by behaviour. An effective moral order must give society self-discipline, so that the great majority of differences are settled without going to law or calling in the police. But once the moral order is removed, disorder arises and we have to rely far more on the law to settle our differences.

Political correctness is a flimsy alternative

The concept of 'politically correct' behaviour is an attempt to create a substitute for the former Christian moral law. But, compared with the Judeo-Christian heritage, it is a very flimsy device; otherwise we would not have so many cases of sexual harassment. Recent cases show that the law is a very clumsy instrument in dealing with such cases; but at work there are still disciplines which exercise some restraint. Outside work and family there is nothing but the law, and if the family breaks down there is nothing. Looking at the huge housing estates round his city, one chief constable said, 'If there are not a mother and father to keep two children in order, how can a couple of my men keep two thousand in order?'

If we are going to maintain women's rights, then we have to have a society which respects them as part of its carefully taught and deeply held beliefs. Instead we have a strong diet of pornography which treats women as sex objects and then we seem surprised when we find that so many men do not have the self-restraint to ignore it. If we are going to protect children from abuse after they are born, then we need a deeply held belief which makes us want to protect them while they are in the womb. But if we treat them as disposable nuisances when they are in the womb, it is a short step to maltreating them if they are a nuisance when they arrive. And if a woman is a sex object, why not her children?

It seems rather odd to argue that we have to be a permissive and therefore secular society because of the new religions brought in by immigrants when – on the importance of the family – Christians, Jews, Muslims and Sikhs are all on the same side. All believe not only that the family is essential to society and has to be protected, but also that there are absolute values enshrined in written codes. There should be no difficulty about public policies which take account of the religious differences, but are united on the wide areas of general agreement.

Modernism loses its grip

It is small wonder that modern secular society is beginning to lose its grip. This is not all gain for Christians. The Christian can debate with 'modernism', because the argument is still on a rational basis and because, though debased by Darwinism, the ideals which motivate modernism still hold something of the Christian dignity of the individual. But modernism's rejection of the Christian foundations of society has laid it open to the much more damaging theories of post-modernism.

The Christian basis of experimental science

Modernism claims descent from the eighteenth-century 'enlightenment', which was anticlerical and utilitarian. What gave it its popular appeal was Darwinism: the idea that science had proved that there was no God, that we were masters of our fate and that science was both our guide and our instrument. It conveniently ignored the founders of modern science, who were post-Reformation Christians in England, the Netherlands and Protestant France. They limited their new experimental methods to secondary causes – which could be observed, catalogued and tested – believing that they could not and should not enquire into the great primary cause by which everything was created. Science was about practical matters. It should not waste its time over metaphysical theories which could never be proved. All that is on the record, from the pen of the great Francis Bacon, who was their spokesman and populariser.

What are not on the record are the reasons why the scientific method is so firmly rooted in the basic beliefs of the Reformers. Few people today read Calvin's *Institutes* – that great intellectual defence of reformed Christianity – which stripped away all the barnacles of the medieval church and took the reformed church back through the theology of the great Augustine, Bishop of Hippo, to the early fathers and the apostles themselves.

The great theme of the Reformers was the sovereignty of God. They believed that everything came from God, including the created order. Since he was the one and only God, the scientists believed that there would be unity in the natural order. Since he was a God of order, laying down the moral order by which men and women should relate to one another, there would also be order in nature; 'everything after its kind' and so it should be possible to catalogue the order of nature. They also believed that he was a God of reason, since he reasoned – through the teaching of the apostles and prophets and through Jesus Christ – that every human action had its inevitable consequence. So they had to search for cause and effect in nature. They believed that the natural laws would be stable, since God had promised stability after the flood, the last great natural catastrophe. And they believed that the bounty of nature was given to us by a generous God and that – though blighted by the rebellion of men and women – nature was benign and we should discover its laws in order to make use of it, 'for the relief of man's estate'.

The result of the scientific method was the greatest explosion of knowledge in the history of the world. There had been Chinese science, Egyptian science and Islamic science; but none of them had been worked into a soundly based intellectual system like this. Linked to the Puritan ethic of hard work and saving, it also produced the widest explosion of wealth and, as science worked through into medical application, of health too.

'Man is the measure of things'

By the end of the nineteenth century, there was enormous optimism that 'man is the measure of things', and that our destiny was in our own hands. There seemed to be no limit to the advances of science. The steam engine was followed by the petrol engine, the train by the car and, just into the twentieth century, the car by the aeroplane. Universal education would produce a rational population, which would deal with crime and violence. The prophets of the age included the Huxleys, H. G. Wells, Bernard Shaw and the Bloomsbury set, whose Virginia Woolf is an ikon to this day. Not only did the church leaders give way before the tidal wave of popular support for modernism, but those in the church who still held on to its basic beliefs were weakened by a pietistic, inward-looking period. Following the deaths of the great Lord Shaftesbury and Charles Haddon Spurgeon, there was a seventy-year gap while they forgot about the far-reaching social reforms of Shaftesbury and the firm rock of Christian theology which had made Spurgeon such an eminent preacher and leader. The false prophets had a clear run.

It was in forgetting the Christian heritage of science, and especially in forgetting that it is about secondary causes and not about the unprovable first cause, that modernism sowed the seeds of its own destruction. Science without a moral framework is now seen as a danger. The man in the white coat has become a threat. Two world wars and the invention of nuclear weapons have shown that science has as much power for evil as for good. The rising ecological movement has pointed out that there must be moral limits on the use of knowledge; that we must, as Christians also believe, preserve the eco-system and the earth's natural resources for future generations.

Post-modernism

If that had been the only reaction to modernism, it might have been in little danger. But modernism, which thought that by substituting education for the superstition of religion it would produce a benign and self-disciplined society, has discovered that the removal of the belief in a rational Creator produces superstition instead of faith and chaos instead of order. We are fast returning to pagan beliefs in many competing gods, and a disorderly, irrational, unstable and malign universe. There are now horoscopes in all the newspapers. Witches and wizards are with us again, pagan solstices and rituals (though not yet any human sacrifice) and all the superstitions condemned by Moses are now being practised in Britain today.

The intellectual face of this rebellion against modernism is post-modernism. There may be some relief among Christians that the pretensions of modernism are being taken apart. But at least it was rational, even if we did not believe in its rationale. We could and did argue with modernists, for we had the firm basic belief in reason on which to debate. I argued with the President of the Royal Society that I did not find evolution a credible theory and he told me that I was just as entitled, on the evidence, to disbelieve in evolution as he was to believe in it. But post-modernism simply removes the framework of rationality. Its creed is that no one can be certain of anything.

We cannot dive down every alley of post-modernist thought, but we can look at its attitude to human dignity in literature and the arts. Charles Dickens, writing in the mid-Victorian age of faith, gives a human dignity to all his characters. However stupid, covetous, arrogant or evil, they are full-blooded personalities and responsible for all their actions. The same can be said for the cartoons in *Punch*. From its first publication in 1842 until the early 1960s, they too are of real people whom we recognise and can laugh at. But post-modernism scorns the representational. Its genre is chaos and disorder. As we look at the post-modern paintings in the airport departure lounge, we are glad that the plane itself is still designed on the scientific method.

The most damaging dogma of post-modernism is that there is no absolute truth; but it is hard to see how there can be a dogma that there is no dogma. A professor of theology had a student at his lecture who argued that there could be no one absolute truth in a statement; the truth was whatever the hearer themselves made of it. The professor continued to misunderstand what she was saying until she became totally exasperated, when he answered her precisely in her own post-modern terms, 'But that's how I hear you.'

It is not enough to laugh off post-modernism as an intellectual fad, got up by an in-group for their mutual entertainment. It has now entered into the mainstream of everyday language. Although no one could argue it in a court of law and certainly no one could argue it in paying wages or settling debts, it can still muddy the waters of social obligations – like those in marriage and the family – and it turns clear notions of right and wrong into a moral maze. The question is which part of our taut industrial, commercial and democratic system it will weaken next.

The threat to industrial democracy

What is certain is that our industrial democracy cannot stand a loosening of the machinery which drives us. We can have organisations which produce wealth on a scale never dreamed of before, or, alternatively, we can have sloppy language which allows us to say one thing and mean another; but we cannot have both. Industrial democracy depends on the validity of language; on a legal system which distinguishes truth from falsehood; on a commercial system without bribery, in which the lowest bid earns the contract; on an employment system in which people can rely on being paid what they are owed; on an industrial system in which design tolerances are measured to the thousandth of an inch; and on a scientific system on which we can depend for our safety in the air and in the food we eat.

We cannot afford an intellectual leadership which has cut us loose from our moorings and which has lost the respect of ordinary people. If they are told that there are no longer any binding moral rules then, no doubt, a good many will take advantage. But that will not stop us all talking in terms of right and wrong, especially when we or someone near us is hurt. The mugging and even killing of old ladies for the few pounds in their purse has universal condemnation. We are told that there is no longer any moral reason why a man should not run off with a girl thirty years younger; but when a politician does this, it is all over the papers at once. And those who thought they could get away with it find that their actions have removed their dignity and public standing and have put them on the same level as a class of people they despise.

It is extremely dangerous to a democratic system of government to allow itself to be guided by a morality (or lack of it) which the average citizen does not accept. From time immemorial, governments have relied on a commonly accepted moral order, taught by the religious leaders and carrying some religious sanctions, even if only the disapproval of society. It is not possible to have a social order without some underlying moral order. It is possible to change the moral order, as pagan Rome changed to the Christian faith or as Northern Europe changed at the Reformation from Catholic to Lutheran and Calvinist. But we are trying something much more far-reaching and very much riskier.

The great weakness of a moral system invented by intellectuals is that it has no grass-roots organisation. Even today Christian churches, not to mention the synagogues and mosques, are spread across the country. People meet at least once a week to listen to preachers and teachers, have Sunday (or other) schools to teach their next generation, have a vast and widely read literature and have the mutual reinforcement of a strong social life. This may affect only 10 per cent of the population, but that is more than the crowds who go to football matches. It is far more than those who go to political meetings. In Easter 1994 I spoke across the country at seminars in seven of the nine Spring Harvest/Word Alive conferences. When I reported to my parliamentary colleagues that the average attendance at the seminars was a thousand, they found it hard to believe. Twenty at a political meeting is good going!

It is one thing for the humanists to knock down the existing morality. It is not too difficult to persuade people that it is quite all right to throw over moral restraint. But though, of course, the intellectuals condemn violence, they cannot protect society against it. In the pubs the general view is that the powers that be are soft on violence, that the streets are no longer safe and that those who harm others should be given a taste of their own medicine. The danger is not that the humanists will win in the long run; the danger is that the weak restraint of political correctness will snap and we will have a political backlash which will sweep away democracy itself.

Christian respect for the dignity of the individual

At its very basic level, humanist teaching, both modern and post-modern, diminishes respect for human beings. The Christian teaching is that each individual is divinely created, personally accountable to God the Creator for all that we do, say and think. That applies to the poorest and richest, the cleverest and the dimmest; to the mentally and physically disabled as well as to the fit. It teaches that each of us can and should pray directly to the Creator of the universe, who hears and cares and answers each of us individually. It tells us not only that we should not harm our neighbours, but that we should care for them as much as we care for ourselves. It gives husbands the obligation to love their wives as Christ loved the church, and tells fathers not to exasperate their children.

The Christian message brings a response which does not depend on race or culture. I asked an Albanian girl in her early twenties how she had become a Christian. She said that she had come across 'this book' in a library, and at the beginning it was about 'this incredible man' whose ideas she admired. Then she came to a bit about the family, where it spelt out how husbands and wives should treat each other and how they should treat their children and how their children should treat them. She said, 'I decided that that was absolutely right, that's how it should be.' 'This book' turned out to be the New Testament and the 'bit about the family' was Paul writing to the church at Colosse.

But if everyone is taught that men and women are no more than a highly developed species of animal, that there is no divine Creator and no moral law except what we invent from time to time for ourselves, then we may talk of the dignity of men and women, but we mean something different and we make each other a great deal more vulnerable to the pressures of abuse and exploitation. Though these things cannot be proved in a chemistry laboratory, there is certainly a correlation between the abandonment of the Christian view of men and women as very special creatures made in the image of God, and the extraordinary rise in crimes of violence against the person.

Nor does the humanist social construct avoid obvious contradictions. I served on Lord Longford's Commission on Pornography, which followed the abolition of censorship and the appearance of all kinds of pornography in the high-street newsagents. As well as bishops and rabbis, the members also included some leading humanists, who were as horrified as we were at the way in which pornography treated women as no more than sex objects. We had some limited success; explicitly pornographic magazines were removed to the top shelves and policemen – including one or two senior officers who had been taking bribes from Soho pornographers – were put in prison.

But humanism, as opposed to the humanist members on our committee, did not seem to be able to draw a line which allowed freedom of speech but did not allow the sale of photographs

16

which treated woman as sex objects. Since that time a huge trade has grown not only in pornographic videos, but in videos of violence, which degrade the whole human race. A generation ago we were challenged to prove that there was a correlation between pornography and rape and violence. Today the correlation is clear. The humanist doctrine of 'political correctness' says that women should not be molested, but that is a poor and ineffective substitute for the Christian moral order.

The rise of the drug culture also shows the same lack of respect for the dignity of the human being. Christians believe that God made us rational and responsible beings and that we have no right to blow the minds which he has given us and to become dependent on the drugs which remove our rationality.

I once visited a government-run drug rehabilitation centre and they clearly did an excellent job on detoxification. But, though they could get people off drugs, they could not, as a government organisation, tell those who were cured why they should stay off. And the temptation to get hooked again was very powerful. So they tended to argue for decriminalisation. If their clients could get the drugs on prescription from a chemist, then they would not have to commit a crime to get the money and the drug barons would be out of business.

This ignores the danger of a person high on drugs to the rest of the community. Drugs are addictive and people will take them when they are on duty as well as when they are off, putting at risk passengers, other road-users, customers and those who work alongside them. We all depend on each other's habit of discipline, and those who lose their rationality and self-discipline on a job or on the road are a danger to others.

The drug centres which I have visited and which are run by churches are far freer to give reasons why their clients should stay off drugs. Most church-run drug centres see time spent with them as no more than the beginning of their job. They try to get their clients safely housed when they leave, find them friends who will be around to help and then try to get them back into work.

The least forgivable pushers are those who sell to children. I passed a very angry teenage girl one day, saying to a young man of about twenty, 'You have no right to push them.' He held his hands up and said, 'I don't push, they want them.' She shouted at him and ran away. Later I saw him with two others waiting with a mobile phone, then doing a transaction through the open window of a car which came up, after which they all ran off. I gave a description of the car, people and place to the police, but the same group were at it again when I passed at the same time a few days later, just as the schools closed. There is big money and good organisation, and there must be a limit to what the local police can do.

We are bringing up a generation of children, half of whom have the misery of broken homes. We are taking away any spiritual hope too, and there must be a great temptation for men and women to find their happiness in a chemical fix and to believe those who tell them that drugs are just another form of recreation.

The Christian ideal of the family

We all need the companionship of the family, and children need the guidance and example of parents. We read in the book of Genesis the Creator's verdict that 'It is not good for man to be alone.' Even in a perfect world we were made to live together in families and, until we may leave our family, to live as man and wife and to have our own family, it is good to have a father and mother – also brothers and sisters – who love us and feel responsible for us, so that we are never alone in the world. We also have obligations to and from the extended family of parents, brothers and sisters, grandparents, grandchildren, uncles, aunts, cousins, nieces and nephews. We are naturally gregarious beings and not loners. But the break up of the family is making more and more people live alone. The average size of household has gone down sharply and, as mentioned before, a quarter of the whole population of Britain now live all on their own.

It is, of course, easier to please ourselves if we live alone. But it is not much fun being alone, so we try to make a circle of friends. The Christian has a natural circle in the church, which has an obligation to its lonelier members and to those who do not find it easy to make friends. But I read a piece in the paper which brought home to me how fragile this wider circle is for those who have to find friends for themselves. The writer had lost her diary with all the phone numbers of her circle of friends. This was a catastrophe. She did not want to go to the pubs alone and unless they called her, she had no means of finding them again. Casual friendships, great fun while they lasted, were ephemeral and had vanished into thin air with the phone numbers.

Churches run drop-in centres for those who want someone to talk to, someone to look to for advice and counsel. These counsellors report a great increase in loneliness. We are free to do what we like, but when we do, it seems pointless unless there is someone else around to enjoy it with us. Loneliness leads to depression and counsellors report a lot more of that too.

It is hard to see that the break up of the moral order has added to the sum of human happiness. That was its great attraction but it turns out to be a fraud.

Chapter Two

NEIGHBOURS IN NEED

Though there may be agreement about the statistics, which tell us what has happened, it is far harder to come to agreement on why there has been this slide into social chaos. The churches and missions who are dealing with the human disasters have more right to a hearing than those who are further away, especially those who do not feel that it is their job to deal in moral issues. Down the centuries, the church was the natural place of refuge for those in need and, with the overload on the welfare state, the church has been called back into service.

Not all those we visited had rushed into social care with enthusiasm. There were many ministers who felt that their work was to preach and teach – not, for instance, to house the homeless. We visited one of these, whose church was down by the docks in Aberdeen. He told us,

The down-and-outs used to come to the church door every Sunday night and I told them to go to the social services and that there was nothing I could do to help them. Then one day a boy, instead of going away like the older ones, slipped past us into the church and we went back in, but couldn't find him. Finally we found him under the desk in the vestry, but he pleaded with us that we would not turn him out. So I thought maybe the Lord was speaking to me and telling me that it was our job after all.

They cleared out the cellars, put in some old armchairs, washrooms, a place to make tea and opened their door on to the dockside, from eight at night until eight in the morning. In charge was a burly Scots giant with a pleasant smile but a determined way with him. I asked what happened if there was trouble. He said, 'If there's everr trrouble, I just throw them oot!' There was seldom any trouble.

Others were not so fortunate. One of the first visits was to Liverpool, where there was a church cafe in the heart of the drug trade. But the drug barons didn't like it and after it had been wrecked several times it had to be closed.

Those who are trying to deal with the collapse where it hurts hardest have their views and, since they are actually dealing with the problems, they are entitled to be heard. Over the last few years, as I have gone round, I have listened as they talked not only about what they were doing, but also gave their views on why the people whom they were trying to help have got into difficulties. And over thirty or more visits, there is a fairly clear pattern of cause and effect. I have talked again to eighteen people from a representative cross-section of the projects and asked them for their thoughts.

Children in need

It is perhaps right to start with the needs of the youngest. We visited a project for children in the East Belfast Mission, a Methodist church on the Newtonards Road, in a district at the heart of the Protestant paramilitary area.

The minister, Jim Rae, said that East Belfast has 'high unemployment, a rising number of broken families, mixed-up people and a sense of malaise. Many local people think that the politicians are so concerned with the constitutional issues that there is no one to articulate their feelings, and their views on the lack of social justice are not heard.'

The mission has a drop-in centre, gives lunch to those who need it and has beds for the homeless. But the project we came to see was across the road in a three-storey house, which is open in the late afternoon and evening as a homework club. It aims to give space and quiet to children who live in crowded homes where there is little room and no peace for them to do their homework. There are volunteer teachers to give help, especially to those who are coming up to examinations. This is the only project of its kind which we have seen, and gives a chance for an educational breakthrough for those children without any peace or home support for their work. For those leaving school – or out of work – there is a job club to teach people how to apply and how to make themselves more marketable.

The minister felt that the major problem in his district was

a lack of respect for law and order and no respect for the authority of older people in the local community. The respect for family life has gone too. Increasingly couples live together outside marriage and then drift away from each other. When problems get too great, they drown them in drink and, as a result, alcoholism is a serious problem. But it is a symptom, it is no cure.

In the last generation, neighbours would come out and tell children to behave and the children would listen. There were good citizens like Mollie Taylor, well known in the neighbourhood, and who *was* citizen's rights, writing letters for all who had a problem. There is some of that spirit still left. When the church stood up to the paramilitaries, it got a lot of support.

We visited a sprawling farm near Flint in North Wales, where Edna Speed and her husband take in whole families to keep the family together and avoid the children being taken into care. She was a teacher in the estate in Chester from which most of the families come and she and her husband took the farm when she retired from teaching. We asked when children first hit trouble and she said, 'As soon as they open their eyes, when they are born.' The project has accommodation for fifty-six, including children, mainly at the old farmhouse. It is explicitly Christian and one of the rooms is a chapel.

Val Trice, one of the senior workers, told us,

In the estate outside Chester there is widespread poverty, in sharp contrast to the wealth in the city itself. Many who live there are second-generation unemployed, with no rhythm to the day, no good habits, no guidance about what is right and wrong. They have problems with personal relationships because they come from families where fathers and mothers change partners whenever the music stops. Some children go with one family and some with another and end up with other people's children. So there are a lot of hurts and one huge problem is the feeling of rejection by parents, by partners, and by the community. So they build a hard outer crust, which is very difficult to get through.

A lot of them find it difficult to live for long in any community and spend their time going from place to place, trying to avoid their past, including criminal offences. Sometimes, when the courts catch up, they will give them deferred sentences if there is some monitoring agent, such as this project, to keep them. Some come to the project because they have arrived homeless on the doorstep of the police; some are sent by community health workers, some by doctors. Most of those who come are on the books of the social services, but, since the scandals of child abuse, the social services prefer to refer people to houses under their direct control.

Although the children certainly had a hard crust, this melted as soon as the motherly figure of Edna Speed appeared. They all made a rush for her and wanted to talk to her and to show her their toys, a response to a love which had penetrated to the roughest.

PECAN in South-east London have a course in parenting skills which is in great demand. Simon Pellew comments,

> The problem seems to be a loss of skills in handling bad behaviour. Some people seem confused by clever theories and professionals have lost common sense. Broken families are a contributory factor. If the problems cannot be handled when they are children, even greater problems build up when they are teenagers. The problem starts when children refuse to do what they are told and parents just back away and give up. The problem is made worse by lack of self-discipline in adults. A large part of the problem is that the family no longer seem to talk to each other. Where there is a TV in the children's bedroom, they get used to doing what they

like and their parents do not see much of them. Even if they do not have a separate TV, sitting children in front of TV takes the place of family conversation. What is on TV also has a major role. '*Power-rangers*' influences behaviour.

So the course starts by asking parents, 'What are your rules?' and then, 'What are the consequences of breaking them?' It teaches children how to protect themselves against abuse, to shout for help, to know who is safe and who is not, and that it is OK to talk about what has happened. It helps children cope with bereavement; it helps adopted children to do 'life-story work' to find out who they are. It also prepares children for care, since the care system – with constant moving from one foster parent to another – confuses them. It teaches them to avoid mishandling, physical abuse and sexual abuse.

Children who have parents who do not love each other are in constant tension. When a father leaves, children can misbehave in the hope that their misbehaviour will make Mum call Dad back. Behaviour patterns are worse where there has been a separation; children would sooner have quarrelling parents, whatever the tension.

Teenagers

On three big estates in North Manchester, there is a youth work programme run by Dr Dave Furze and his team, all of whom live on the three estates. Their aim is to help teenagers who are at risk and disadvantaged. Dave Furze told us,

The area has unemployment of 58 per cent – higher on our three estates. A lot of big employers closed down in the early 1980s and any new business has gone to South Manchester, because of the dock and motorway access. The motorway ring missed us out. For a long time the council did not invest – though they have now decided to put in £20 million for refurbishment and have appointed a social programme officer.

The estate has the highest teenage pregnancy rate in

Europe. It has high infant mortality and a high death rate, partly from bad eating habits, partly from bad housing. Fifty per cent of the mothers are single parents, 50 per cent of new births are to unwed mothers and, among the married couples, the divorce rate is high. Many of those teenagers who go on to sixth form soon drop out, as do a large proportion of those who make it to higher education. So the youth unemployment rate is 75 per cent.

Standard-type youth work is very difficult because it is not possible to impose the necessary discipline for indoor activities. The teenagers need minimum restriction and maximum fun. The members of the team (three in each estate) have to make friends with them, to earn the trust which can only be given to a neighbour living on the estate. So each team lives in a house on its estate.

The work is based on a 'street club'. We take the members out in a minibus and a car to a swimming pool, a bowling alley, a 'laser quest' (played in a dark space with obstacles, all players carrying a laser gun and backpack target which registers the hit) or a country park within a radius of twenty miles, where they do orienteering or play wide games (in the military manner with team objectives) or in town, where they do treasure hunts. The teenagers are not in control as they are on their estate and the team do not have to police a building, so there is more equality of status. At some point they have a talk of no more than five minutes, where they have to be quiet. Each talk includes some life skill. It includes Christian morals, the 'big questions' of relationships, the future and 'who am I?' On the way home we stop at a chip shop.

Apart from the street club, there is detached work. This involves going round the area in pairs, talking to whoever is there and making the initial link or relating with someone already known. We talk about what is going on, about the latest football scores, for example. We carry a frisby or football; listen to all that is said, picking up from where they were last time we met them.

They are second- or third-generation unemployed. Their parents get by without a job, so why shouldn't they? They make money illegally and by selling in the local weekly market. They have no work ethic and no role model. They have a low self-worth, so the team need to build their self-esteem and to open their eyes to what they could do if they tried.

A lot of them cannot read properly. Their parents are at the limit of what they can read themselves and see no reason to read with their children. Those coming to the local secondary school at eleven have an average reading age of eight. Some do not even know their alphabet. As a result many do not understand what is going on in the class and become bored; either they create trouble or they skip school. There is now a project of 'reading pals', where they are taken out of normal classes and one of the team will read with them for an hour a day. Local Christians also volunteer in both secondary and primary schools. This has produced a dramatic increase in literacy. Then, when they can understand what is going on in the class, attendance goes up and it improves their quality of life.

The estates were grey and dreary places, with nothing constructive for any of the teenagers to do. There was very little, if any, police presence and when we were there, there had been a great deal of thieving and joy-riding in stolen cars. One boy had been killed when run over by a car driven by another boy who was incapable of controlling it.

Teenage homelessness

Like the project in Manchester, the Glasgow City Mission is also very mobile, going where the people are, rather than expecting them to come to the mission. Graeme Clark told us,

The main cause of teenage homelessness is the arrival of a stepfather. Since the withdrawal of unemployment allowance for sixteen- to eighteen-year-olds, he refuses to bear the cost of someone he regards as a pain in the neck. They live in a grey community with nothing to do, no colour to life and easily get on to drugs, when their behaviour and personal relationships deteriorate rapidly. That may trigger their exit or it may follow.

In places like Drumchapel, on Clydeside, employment would help to resolve the problem and there are church projects, funded by the Manpower Services Commission, to try to make people – including mentally disabled – employable and to get back their self-confidence.

Graeme Clark had run the Fife Interchurch Association project, which gave woodwork, metalwork and computer training. He told us that these had a remarkable success in finding people full-time jobs, as had the Buckhaven scheme of the Church of Scotland in Fife. But MSC funding was withdrawn.

One unique outreach to homeless boys was based on a Baptist church near Cardiff. It seemed to depend very much on the personality of Barry Lakin, who ran it from an office just inside the glass doors of the church, opening straight off the street. He set out to find landladies who would take the homeless boys, assuring them that he would not land them with a teenage hooligan. The church gave the landladies a bond of £100 against any damage or arrears and Barry Lakin told them that if there were any trouble – if, for instance, a boy came in drunk – they should ring for him and, day and night, he would come straight round and deal with him. He said,

The problem with the boys is that they do not know how to behave and I have to teach them.

One of the causes of homelessness is unemployment in the family. There is, perhaps, not enough to pay off the mounting arrears of debt. When the boy leaves school, there is resentment against a son who lies around in bed all day and contributes nothing. Sometimes physical cruelty drives the boy out, sometimes it is just verbal abuse. But more often it is the break up of the family which is the trigger. A new boyfriend has taken their mother's attention and loyalty and the house is no longer home.

Barry Lakin has helped to find new jobs, but it is not easy with little employment on offer. Some, finding that the dirty washing

27

just stayed on the floor where they dropped it, got lonely and drifted back home. Some got into trouble and went to prison. Some, in their twenties, got jobs and made a go of their life.

One of the mainstream charities which provides for the homeless is Adullam Homes, based in the Midlands. Rob Taylor, their director, told me that they look after young people who have just come out after being in care, and have special refuges for women and their dependents who are vulnerable because of domestic violence. He said, 'The young find it hard to rise above their background.' As with the others, he said that the main reason for homelessness among the young is either that they cannot get on with their stepfather or that they are not wanted.

They try to teach those who need them the skills of living in a family, But,

> We find a great increase in a sense of hopelessness; people find it hard today to see a constructive future for themselves in society. Christian values have now gone. There is no other authority which is respected and no consistent world-view, so we are now in a stage of social disintegration. Yet, there is a God-shaped hole which has to be filled. People are longing for some significance and meaning in life. They do have values, but they pick and mix them; there is no coherence. They see some offences as revolting but would, for instance, argue that burglary only deprived insurance companies. Many young have never known work and for those who have, it has been intermittent.

He added that the welfare state seems to have created a culture of dependency, with an economic trap where the step from welfare to work is too great. 'There needs to be a shallower half-step. There is great pressure too on the social services from the much greater demands made on them by current social behaviour.'

Teenage prostitutes

The Glasgow City Mission also does a work for prostitutes, which has been based in a disused pub in the red light district. They are now well ahead for a bigger, better-equipped drop-in centre. The appearance of younger girls made the work more urgent. Linked to this will be a new short-stay crisis care house for women who want to get away. The initial cause of young girls going on the streets is probably abuse at home but, once there, the main motive is to find money for drugs, most of them being on heroin.

Another work for young prostitutes in London finds a strong link with drug addiction, and one problem strengthens the other. The prostitute needs drugs because of her lifestyle and earnings as a prostitute to pay for the drugs. Drugs have a stronger hold on the younger girls now on the streets than they did on the old generation of prostitutes, which was almost drug-free. The girls seem mainly to have taken to the streets when they have been thrown out of their homes or when they leave after a row. They come to the city and are picked up by the pimps.

Urban Action Manchester also has a work for prostitutes. Most have suffered child abuse or been on drugs. Some are students, desperate for money to make up tight grants. Their project aims to have a drop-in centre shortly, and meanwhile a middle-aged woman helper takes a car round the streets with sandwiches and hot drinks.

Adullam Homes also look after the rehabilitation of drug addicts. They find that it needs three or four attempts before those hooked on drugs can finally get free. They have specially adapted housing for people living with HIV.

Helping unemployed to find work

There are now quite a number of projects which try to overcome the feeling of hopelessness by helping people to regain their self-esteem and giving them the skill to make successful job applications. The role model to which most of these projects look is PECAN in Peckham, South London, which has a staff of thirty-two, most engaged in helping the unemployed.

Simon Pellew, who runs the project said,

Unlike most similar projects, we go out and knock on doors to find people who might like our help, but have not heard about it. Since we knock on ten thousand doors a year, this is labour-intensive work. The neighbourhood has the highest density of population in Europe; it lacks 'defensible space' and social control, and there is a very high degree of deprivation. Twenty per cent of the unemployed men have been out of work for three years.

Those who knock on doors need to be trained in door-to-door selling. The important part is the first few words. They usually find that half the people are out and half of those who are in are not interested. About 13 per cent of those interested finally turn up. But of those who go through the course, 40 per cent come because we knocked on their doors and the remaining 60 per cent find out from our stall at the benefit office.

A quarter of those who come have degrees! Half are Africans, most of whom have higher education qualifications and not all are young; 80 per cent are over twenty-six. They are taught where and how to look for jobs. They are helped to frame CVs and, in order to train them in how to do a good interview, we persuade local employers from nearby churches to come in and give them an interview as a dry run.

But a large part of the job is to build their self-esteem, to make them see what gifts, skills and experience they have really got. A heavy goods vehicle driver who had a back injury could not drive again and was unqualified for anything else. But when pressed on his spare-time activities to find his hidden talent, he said that he was the secretary of the Peckham Tropical Fish Breeding Association. So clearly he did have talent for other jobs!

The reason for the high unemployment in Southwark is the huge move out of South-east London in the 1970s and the move of the labour-intensive London docks to the container port at Tilbury. And the nearby City of London looks to the suburbs for its recruiting.

The success rate of those who finish the PECAN course is over 70 per cent and other similar projects seem to have the same level of success.

Training for jobs

Although there are quite a number of projects to help people find jobs, there are fewer church agencies which can train people for work and almost none which can themselves create jobs. The Bethany Trust in Edinburgh is trying to make a training project create jobs as well.

Alan Berry of the Bethany Christian Trust told me,

> We are planning a four-year project to give training in joinery, building, landscape gardening and horticulture. It will train twenty people for a year. We will also build houses, so that the project looks after both training and accommodation and gives real jobs, and we are negotiating with colleges of further education for a franchise which would pay for the training.

They are also running a course to help people find jobs, based on the PECAN course in Peckham and they now have a 60 to 70 per cent success rate in finding jobs or really useful training. It is much more difficult for those who have had no job for over three years.

Alan Berry said,

> Unemployment is much more evident today. There are beggars in the streets, people selling the *Big Issue*. Morality has dropped, with far more teenage pregnancies, and marriage breakdown is now an epidemic. The most common reason for the young to be on the streets is a row with their stepfather. The rise in single mothers increases the need for more houses, but there are none. There are too many latchkey kids and the young have to struggle against tides which are unparalleled in history.

Afro-Caribbean churches

Projects like PECAN, which are in the middle of the ethnic mix of South-east London, cater for all comers, but there are areas where the Afro-Caribbean churches are strong and feel that they have to look after the special needs of their own people. Rev. J. B. Corbett said that the United Evangelical Project was set up for the Afro-Caribbean churches when, after riots in Birmingham, there were indiscriminate arrests and the Afro-Caribbean families came to their churches to try to get help in finding out where their sons had gone and to get legal aid in defending them.

Arising out of that there is now a prison-link work, with a 'return programme' to get those returning to society into jobs. There is also a law centre, which does a lot of work on debt counselling. People did not know their social service entitlements and did not ask for benefits, so they went to loan offices where they were offered high-interest credit without all the formalities of the social services.

Among the Afro-Caribbeans there had also been a baby explosion when girls became pregnant after learning from the council that this was the only way they could get a house. But then they got into debt because they picked up furniture on hire purchase and found that they could not pay. They had no idea of the rate of interest which they were paying. The centre is now setting up a credit union and hopes that they can offer loans at no more than 6 per cent.

The project has male hostels for the young who have problems of mental health and for the old. They find that the social services lifestyle imprisons the old, the sick and the senile so they are setting up a united church housing association for senior citizens.

Rev. J. B. Corbett commented, 'Our main social problems come from men walking out of partnerships as soon as children arrive and from broken marriages. The young have difficulties in relating to their parents and to pastors. Some become Rastafarian in protest. So we have a training programme for parents and children.'

Debt

The Afro-Caribbean churches are not alone in facing the problem of debt. In Cardiff there is a debt counselling centre, tactfully concealed at the back of a church bookshop. Andrew Buchanan-Smith, who runs it, said,

This is an area with a lot of absolute poverty. There are occasional cases of extortion, but mainly our work is to give legal advice on what can be negotiated with a creditor. The Office of Fair Trading has now given a licence to the 'shopacheque' (a form of credit) which carries an annual interest rate of 100 per cent. The main cause of debt is poverty. The cooker breaks down and they have to have something to cook on, so they take out a loan for a new cooker because the DHSS Social Fund does not cover it.

The level of debt tends to increase. The lending company sends in a neighbour to have a cup of tea with a woman on a Friday when her husband is down at the pub and the borrower is on her own. If the money is not there, the friendly neighbour suggests a 'roll-up loan' and the borrower does not calculate the weekly cost of the new interest. So the debt goes on mounting.

This project is trying to set up a local credit union, so that good neighbours can look after one another at a minimal rate of interest and avoid the mounting burden of interest.

There is a similar debt centre in Bristol, run by Martin Green. It is also in a poor area. He told me,

The reasons why most people get into debt which they cannot repay are low incomes, being on benefit too long, or the fact that payment for insecure manual work is getting lower and lower. The proportion of people on less than half the national income has gone up from 14 per cent of the population in 1979 to 24 per cent today.

A lot of people are illiterate and do not know their legal rights to benefit. When the gas, water and electricity companies threaten to disconnect, people in need can appeal; but not knowing how to appeal, they borrow. The rates of interest can be extremely high. The APR for a 'shopacheque' can be cripplingly high.

The debt collectors usually come round just after the weekly dole cheque has been collected. If they find difficulty in getting payment, they often offer a 'roll-over loan' and the debtor – not realising that the interest payments would then be impossible and that they should and could get advice on an arrangement to pay off – just accept the additional loan as part of the necessity of the kind of life they lead.

We ask debtors who come for advice to write down all that they owe, then to put down their income and the minimum amount they need to live on. It is then possible for us to work out a schedule of repayments over a period, which is put to the creditor as a cheaper alternative than a court order.

Martin Green said that there was now a local initiative for a credit union and it was estimated that it could lend at 12.7 per cent.

Counselling the confused

It is small wonder that our age of moral confusion is just too much for a great many people, who find themselves disoriented and depressed and greatly in need of help and advice. One such centre is the Light House in Coventry, a Christian-based counselling service for the whole community, with five paid staff and twenty-one volunteers. It does not push a Christian message, but 'You can't counsel without something of yourself and what you believe coming across.' David Depledge of the centre told me,

The greatest problem is that relationships between people are breaking down, starting with the first husband/wife relationship, then going on to the second, third and fourth relationship. The man complains, 'Her children are always getting in my way.' There are also a lot of women with low self-esteem which makes them take great offence at minor slights, which a more confident person would ignore.

Major personal problems are unfaithfulness of the spouse; people putting ambition and other work pressure before relationships; and sexual abuse, of boys as well as girls. People say that though time helps, it can't take away the pain of abuse and often they blame themselves. 'It must have been my fault.' They have to be convinced that the fault was not with them or something they have done but with the abuser.

There is a counselling centre in another city, with a small staff and 100 volunteers trained in the centre to the standards of the Association of Christian Counsellors. People are referred by doctors, social workers, churches and friends.

They told me that 20 per cent of their clients have marital or other relationship problems; 20 per cent have an identity crisis, a feeling of alienation from society. Many suffer damage from the present pressures of life and the demands of work and have not learnt how to organise their lives and to give enough time to their family. They said that a great many were abused as children and come in their early twenties. Over half have a church background and the rest do not. Thirty to forty years ago they would have been helped through these problems by their family, but now they live isolated lives and have no one to go to near at hand.

Prisoners and their families

The British prison population has gone up by 50 per cent since the 1970s and the Prison Fellowship keeps in touch with prisoners and their families during the period of sentence and afterwards. Robin Scott, local director of the Prison Fellowship in Belfast, told me that their volunteers visit the families of prisoners, arrange transport to the prison for visits and for those who cannot go out themselves, they drive to the shops and take the children away on holiday. A recent project took five families away for a holiday together. The volunteers visit prisons under the auspices of the prison chaplain. With those who want to talk, they share the Christian message, and for those who ask there is a discipleship course and, naturally, the formation of friendships.

When prisoners are released, they see them into accommodation, helping, if need be, to find basic furniture. With high unemployment, it is not easy to find them jobs, though there have been notable successes. They try to arrange training and further education. They raise money by deputation work to churches, especially churches in the community from which the prisoners come. Although a great majority of the prisoners are paramilitaries, there are also those known as ODCs or 'ordinary decent criminals'. Some of the ODCs get into crime through poverty, but the great majority have a background of broken homes.

Adullam Homes, based in Birmingham, also work with prisoners. Their main work is to provide homes for ex-prisoners when they come out. They find that if ex-prisoners can keep straight for a month, they are unlikely to re-offend.

Drugs

Staff at one drug rehabilitation centre told me that most drug offenders are starting younger and many do so because they came from broken families or ones where there was some form of abuse from alcohol- or drug-dependent parents or from a step-parent. Simple peer pressure brings some teenagers on to drugs, thinking that they are as safe as the alcohol their parents drink.

Those who come to the centre have usually had a crisis. Drugs have become the centre of their lives, have got them into crime and into ill health; they have lost all their proper friends, their family, partner and children, their job and self-respect and a crisis has brought them sharply to a decision to try to throw off the habit.

The problem about coming off drugs is that they were the centre of the user's life and now there is nothing there, so their whole life has to be changed. That is the job of rehabilitation. Some walk out during the programme, so there is not a high success rate. Some go back to prison again. Most men in another drug rehabilitation centre we visited had picked up the habit in prison. But there are successes. In a rehabilitation centre in Swansea, the director had been on drugs once himself, but had been completely cured and that had given him the vision and incentive to help others.

Aids

The ACACIA project (Aids Care, Compassion in Action) looks after about seventy-five people with HIV/Aids in their own homes. Besides bringing much needed companionship, the helpers do the shopping and decorate, and a trained nurse does a night-sit for those near to death. There are opportunities, if asked, to share the Christian faith. The gay community are very supportive.

I talked to Rachel Shearer, who was in charge of the project in Manchester. She had originally been on a project for drug users and prostitutes. There were some prostitutes who were HIV-positive and she saw that there was a gap in Christian work and felt a calling to fill it. She found the area of care for Aids patients a spiritual desert. She said,

> Part of the work is with those who are recovering from the shock of finding that they are HIV-positive. They know in their minds that they have another ten to twelve years of life and that we all have a limited life span. But knowing for certain that they will die prematurely is a shock and they want to know what will happen when they do die.

But the greater part of the work is with those who are now suffering with Aids. Half of them are alone, many deserted by family and partners. Those who have stayed with partners dying of Aids have to go out to work.

Most of the work is mundane – doing the shopping, making meals, washing clothes – but it is also about companionship. They know that ACACIA is a Christian organisation and many say they do not want to talk about the Christian faith, but 95 per cent do talk about the spiritual side of their lives. Quite a few have been Christians and want to recommit themselves to the faith. Some, quite dramatically, become Christians. One had a real vision of the cross and afterwards was not afraid of dying. 'I'll go when God wants me.' Some come to church, though worried about whether the church will welcome them. Quite a few take the Alpha course (for those who want to become Christians).

Most of the referrals come from the NHS and from doctors, and the project keeps in close touch with the social services, which helps with its funding. ACACIA has also built good relationships with the secular Aids organisations. It is part of the job of volunteers to pass on their vision of the work to the churches, and there is a monthly prayer meeting for those who want to support the work. Each volunteer has to have their church leaders behind them. There are twenty volunteers who give two to three days a week and there have been three full-time staff, though now it is down to one but, with the increase of the number of referrals and the paperwork which that involves, there needs to be four.

A lot of volunteers are unsuitable, since they do not know what they are letting themselves in for and do not have the special mix of qualities which is needed. Volunteers are given special training on social services courses, on the facts of HIV/Aids, on the process of death, on helping people who are dying, on appropriate reaction and responses, and on bereavement. There is an emotional and spiritual web, where everything interconnects.

Conclusion

If there is one message which comes out loudly and clearly, it is the disastrous effect on British society of the break up of the family. Nearly every new problem has its roots there. And, though most of these projects are in needier areas of our cities, there is no reason to believe that there are not the same problems in wealthier areas, though like their rubbish they are better concealed. From the nation's first family to the most deprived, the break up of the family hits every class, and as the counselling projects tell us, so does the personal disorientation, confusion and depression. Drugs are everywhere and far more money is pilfered by the scams of the rich than by 'ordinary decent criminals'!

But there is a lethal cocktail of unemployment on top of family breakdown. It is that which is so damaging and so potentially explosive for the social structure of British society.

Chapter Three

THE FAMILY –
THE CORNERSTONE OF SOCIETY

What has gone wrong with marriage?

If the break up of the family is one of the disasters of our time, is there anything which can be done about it? Is it some secular trend which we cannot wish away or alter? Has it something to do with the improvement of the position of women which will work out when men come to terms with it? Is it something to do with the high rate of unemployment among men, or with the extra pressures which are now placed on those who have escaped downsizing at the cost of doing other people's work as well as their own?

Clearly there are changes in society which put pressures on marriage. But previous generations have had their pressures too. When life was shorter and illness more lethal, many a widow struggled on to bring up a family all on her own, or, as in Jane Austen's *Mansfield Park*, the heroine was sent off to live with her aunt, uncle and cousins. Dickens' Oliver Twist was an orphan. But the family seems to have survived the industrial revolution, war, famine and pestilence better than it has survived the last thirty years of unparalleled health and prosperity. The factor X could not have destroyed so many families in a brief thirty years were it a purely external factor. It must be something in us which was not there before.

Half a century ago, there was little sign of the family losing its hold on our hearts and minds. When peace came to Europe after six devastating years of war, Winston Churchill stood on the Whitehall balcony with the King and Queen and took the cheers of the crowds packed around the cenotaph below. Yet very shortly afterwards there was a general election and those same crowds threw him out of office. The war in the Far East was not yet over and Conservative election posters had shown Churchill with bulldog determination over the caption, 'Give us the tools and we will finish the job'. But the Labour poster showed a young father at the garden gate, waving goodbye to his wife and two children as he left home for work. That was what the people wanted: to be a happy couple with a home and small garden, a couple of children and a job.

Half a century on that poster would seem too corny to be true. Yet there are still people like that. And there are those who want to be like that. It may be that half the couples who marry today will be divorced; but they do not set out with that intention. They live in the hope that, for them, it will turn out all right. They believe the promises they make to each other. All the wedding guests – well, most of them anyhow – wish them well. And most of those who take partners without getting married hope that it will work out, that they can manage all right without the formal vows and all that formal wedding fuss.

The Christian ideal

So the Christian ideal of a secure and lasting relationship is what most people want. It is not that we think the ideal is not worth having; it is not that we want it to fail; it is that the way we live today makes its achievement more difficult, failure far easier. We think that we can achieve a firm and lasting marriage without the tiresome disciplines and when we find that we do need them, the damage is already done.

One of the age-old disciplines used to be that the man needed to have the permission of the girl's father before he asked her to marry him. Some cultures, of course, go further than this and insist that marriages are arranged by the parents of both bride and bridegroom.

At a summer school for Christian students, the Japanese girl told the Californians that in Japan – where parents arranged their children's marriages – there was no divorce, while in California – where sons and daughters ignored their parents and chose for themselves – the divorce rate was 50 per cent. Students from other countries said that there was no need to go to either extreme; the fifth commandment told children to honour their parents and so they had a duty at least to consult them and to listen to what they had to say.

It is certainly no part of Christian teaching that a daughter is the property of her parents to be given away against her will, or that a son must marry the girl who carries the largest dowry. But parents have a duty of care for their children, including wise and unselfish advice on a marriage partner, given, if it is to be effective, against a long background of mutual love and respect between parent and child.

Marriage and the creation of a family is not, in the words of the marriage service, to be undertaken hastily or unadvisedly. Real love, shown in mutual devotion, is a major factor in overcoming these strains; but the Christian faith also provides a framework for marriage in which the strains and stresses can be resolved. If there is no framework, it is far harder to resolve all the conflicts which are bound to arise.

That does not fly in the face of the ideal of romantic love. It needs more than cold compatibility to hold a marriage together through thick and thin. There has to be real mutual respect and the willing self-sacrifice which distinguishes love from lust. The Anglican wedding service, which gives procreation of children as the purpose of marriage, is too utilitarian. Love comes first and children may or may not follow. Love continues when the children have gone away. And true love grows, so that each year is better than the year before.

But the choice of a marriage partner has to be serious, because it is for life. So marriage via sexual relations outside marriage is a faulty start. There can be no such thing as a 'trial marriage', since marriage gives the solid framework of security in which no problem can lead to a final breach and all problems have to be worked through together. Promiscuity cannot give the security of marriage and because of that, cannot be a 'trial marriage'.

The extended family

The extended family is part of the framework of Christian marriage. The Christian wedding (and that of other religions) is the forum not only for the pledges of the bride and bridegroom, but also of the extended families on both sides to recognise and support the marriage in every way they can. It may sound rather grand and independent to say that the relationship is an entirely independent affair between two people, but that assumes that they can overcome all difficulties without any help; and experience does not bear that out. Today we expect too much of the nuclear family.

This does not mean, as it does in some religions and cultures, that the bridegroom's family, for instance, dominate the marriage. The Christian believes that, in Christ's words, 'A man shall leave his father and mother and shall cleave to his wife.' But it does mean that parents have to be on call. Especially when the children arrive, the wife needs her mother's help, support and advice – the reason for all the old 'mother-in-law' jokes. But sons also need fathers, and, speaking for myself, fathers-in-law. The support of brothers and sisters can also help to spread the load of small children in the nuclear family and see them through the crises of bereavement. Again, speaking for myself, brothers-in-law are a great support.

It is not just for the bad times that we need help. There is a great resource of enjoyment in the wider family. It is a group whom you have known and who have known you over long years, with whom you can share memories and give and take ideas within the intimacy of the family circle as you could not elsewhere. And the next generation have a port of call when they are in a strange city. It is a very sharp contrast to the loneliness of the modern world.

The nuclear family – parents and children – should always be able to look for support to the extended family – grandparents, uncles, aunts and cousins and, sometimes, to great-uncles, great-aunts and second cousins too. This is a circle of privileged access. When children need a second opinion, or someone not involved in the disciplinary process of the home, they can go to an uncle, aunt or grandparent. Grandparents often have time when parents are hard pressed and can draw on a much longer time-span of experience.

The extended family carries obligations too, which in today's hard materialistic mood are often neglected. Poorer and more primitive societies find it incredible that, instead of looking after the elderly members of our families, we park them out in institutions where we may or may not go to visit them. In my days as a politician I often went round old folks' homes and, while some were bright and cheerful, with a lot of banter and laughter, too many seemed to turn their charges into zombies, in homes which I found immensely depressing.

It is true that the elderly may need special attention and the very elderly, like children, cannot be left alone for long. But they do bring an extra dimension into the home and it is good for the oldest and youngest generations to spark off against each other. My wife's mother lived with us or with her other daughter until she died aged ninety-two. My mother lived round the corner under the eyes of my sister, leaving her own home to live with her for the last few months before she died aged eighty-six. They looked after us when we were vulnerable; we should do the same for them. There is a wisdom which comes with age and a disinterestedness which comes when the struggles of life are over. Most cultures have respected this, as our own used to do.

Christian marriage – permanent and monogamous

Christian teaching is that, in sexual union, a man and a woman have become one in a divinely recognised union and 'what God has joined, let not man separate'. That is why Christian marriage is monogamous, and why no one married to more than one wife can hold office in a church.

In polygamy no wife is an equal partner and even the latest wife is vulnerable to whoever follows. Of course, our Muslim friends accuse us of 'serial polygamy'. While they continue to look after every wife they have married, we turn out the old wife whenever we take a new one. So, in their view, our laws are harder on women than theirs.

Christ allowed only one cause of divorce. If one party broke the 'one flesh' by committing adultery, the other party was free.

When he was asked why, if that were so, Moses allowed divorce, he said, 'For the hardness of your hearts Moses allowed divorce, but from the beginning it was not so.' He is drawing a distinction between the moral law, which is unchangeable, and the civil law, which has to be adjusted to what can be enforced. Without a legal process, men would still throw out their wives, who would then be legally unprotected. In a hard-hearted society there have to be laws which regulate the ending of marriages; but they should not be so easy that they actually diminish the protection.

Happiness is subjective and it is not possible to award percentage points to those who have married one husband or wife and stuck by them as compared with those who have engaged in serial polygamy. But every story of polygamy in the Bible is a story of disaster – from Abraham's concubine, through the rape, murder and rebellion of David's sons to the folly of Solomon's son Rehoboam, who lost most of his father's great kingdom as soon as he succeeded him. It is my impression, from long life with a great many friends of all kinds, that husbands and wives who have stuck together are a great deal happier than those who have not.

The importance of the role model

The best contribution of Christians to the permanence of marriage is to set an example, so it is especially sad that marital breakdown has now penetrated the churches and even to clergy and ministers. But that should only make us redouble our efforts to make marriage work. It is especially important for Christian couples never to bear a grudge.

Forgiveness, central to the Christian faith, is also central to marriage. Paul tells us all, not only husband and wife, to make it up before bedtime, 'Let not the sun set on your anger.' The duty to forgive is central to the Christian faith. It is at the centre of the Lord's Prayer: 'forgive us our debts as we have also forgiven our debtors.' If we believe that God forgave us, we must also forgive others. The refusal to carry forward grudges and resentment, the practice of finishing each day with a clean sheet, stops the growth of any division before it has a chance to get hold. It closes that crack of resentment and bitterness before they give justification for the dangerous liaisons which prise it open until it is a yawning gulf.

Safeguards

In the days when Britain had a large navy, it used to be said that there was a navy wives' grapevine which always found out, despite strict official secrecy, when their husbands' ship was due and in which port; so they were all there on the quayside waiting and making quite sure that their husbands did not get into the wrong company after a long spell at sea.

Today it is not so easy for either husbands or wives. The old safeguards have been swept away. Men and women not only work together, they travel together and stay in the same hotels, married and single. There is endless sexual titillation in magazines, in the pornographic videos which are shown on the film channel in every hotel bedroom and the temptation and opportunity are higher than ever before, even for those who want to keep their marriage vows.

I like the advice given by the old Canadian professor to his ordinands after graduation. 'One day a very pretty young woman will come into your vestry. Keep the door open and show her into a chair, but stay your side of the desk. She will tell you a long sad story and you will be very sorry for her; sound sympathetic, but stay your side of the desk; finally she will weep; do not put your arm round her, hand her a tissue, give her sound advice, say goodbye and still stay your side of the desk.'

It is not so easy when men and women are colleagues and a great many divorces start with colleagues at work going over the line before they realise it. Situations can arise when we least expect them and, with the removal of social guidelines, it is as well for Christians to have our personal guidelines clear in our minds. Some people keep their office doors open, try to be with third parties on long journeys and in hotels, and always keep in close touch with their spouses. Staying sober and away from office parties is also found to be helpful!

It is easy to mock this old-fashioned carefulness; but, even if they were not tempted, the removal of guidelines has left men vulnerable to allegations of sexual harassment which, with no witnesses, they are unable to refute. But 'affairs' so often start, even in churches, when two people working together find that they have stepped over an invisible line and do not know how to get back.

Adultery is not glamorous, it is sordid. As we know from the most spectacular divorce cases, it demeans those involved, and they never really recover the respect in which they were once held. And, as the causes of divorce remain with the divorcees in the next partnership, they find that 'the fault, dear Brutus, is not in our stars, but in ourselves'.

Commitment versus freedom

The most powerful argument for divorce is that it frees people from an intolerable bondage which would otherwise last for the rest of their lives. The question is whether divorce at will makes for greater happiness than a commitment for life does. This is not capable of experimental proof, which needs absolutely similar substances subjected to different tests. So it is not possible to say that the 50 per cent of marriages now severed by divorce represent intolerable marriages from which the partners have now been happily released. We have to look for general probabilities instead.

A couple bound in lifelong partnership are not only likely to have taken more care before committing themselves to each other, but they know that every disagreement has to be settled, so they are more likely to patch up quarrels before they go too far. They are more likely to work at marriage, to try to do things together which both can enjoy, to avoid whatever the other cannot stand, to come to a mutual agreement on how to educate and bring up children. And, above all, their complete security in the partnership makes it easier for them to commit themselves to each other whole-heartedly and not to feel the need to hold back. There were a great many marriages of earlier days which went through crises which today would have shattered them, but which then pulled through to achieve a happy and contented relationship.

That is far less likely to happen today where there is reduced commitment, either because they are 'partners' and not legally married or because there is now no final barrier to the spouse who wants a divorce from the other. The result is that there is now no longer the need to make it up or to compromise because, in one way or another, the marriage must be made to work. Today any quarrel can become the last straw, the occasion of going out with someone more sympathetic; and it soon comes the point of no return where quarrels are not made up because each quarrel helps to build up the justification for their case that the marriage is not going to work out.

Women bear the brunt

It is especially hard on the women. Every instinct they have makes them want to look after their children and the pressure to hold the marriage together is on them. The great majority of single parents are mothers. It is the man who has walked out. So, if a mother is to keep the father at home, she has to give in to his wishes far more than he to hers. In the old days it was the mistress who said, 'I have to do whatever he wants.' Now the wife and mother finds herself in the same position. Today's new freedom looks very one-sided. So there is a growing feeling among some women that life is better without a man anyhow.

With growing education and emancipation, women are not willing to put up with neglect and bad treatment. They can always earn their own living and pursue their own career. That feeling is another dissolvent of marriage as an institution. But a solution which drives a wife into loneliness is not good for either spouse.

The children

Another argument for easy divorce is that it is bad for the children to be in an unhappy and quarrelsome home. But if the couple care so much for the children, then it says little for their sense of responsibility or self-control that they cannot stop quarrelling for the sake of the children. In fact it seems now to be accepted that children would prefer a home with quarrels than suffer the loss of one of the parents, and it is clear from schools that children from broken homes are likely to be disturbed and to perform poorly. The last chapter showed that the children were the big losers from divorce, and that the break up of the home with the abdication of parental responsibility leaves a trauma for life even if it does not lead straight to the streets and to drugs.

Marriage is not an institution made only for perfect people who are likely to get on with each other. It is because of all our faults that we need to live in families. Husbands and wives knock the awkward corners off each other and the more we love each other, the more we take the hints in the spirit in which they are given. Our youthful follies may not disappear, but they are a lot less obtrusive. Fathers and mothers stand amazed when they see their newly married sons and daughters taking from their wives or husbands advice which they had scorned to accept from their parents only a few years before!

But parents must do their best to bring up their children in the way they should go while they are still young. The first seven chapters of Solomon's book of Proverbs, as true today as it was three thousand years ago, are addressed by a father to his son. We are given an instinctive love for our children and the warmth of affection which we give them makes the necessary discipline tolerable.

But, in today's pressurised world, we have to give them time – for stories, for games, for expeditions, for travel – we have to share interests with them. We have to find time to listen; to share their excitements, their hopes and fears; to entertain their friends; to sit up with them when they are ill; to encourage them when they are depressed; and to sympathise when they feel hard done by. And, when we are grandparents, we have to do it all over again!

Above all, parents have to be there. There is a lot of talk today about 'quality time'. That seems to mean that we make sure to fit them for a clear hour or so into our busy life. But we never know when they are going to need us badly and when they do, they want to find us on the spot, ready to listen and to comfort, to advise and to cheer. When they are in the difficult years in their teens, then we need the fund of loyalty built up in earlier years, to keep them from the horrors of drugs and all the other follies with which today's permissive society tempts our vulnerable youth. Parents are their role models; the girls need a mother to teach them how to be a woman, the boys a father to teach them how to be a man. It is the lack of a role model which leads to so many aimless and mixed-up children today.

Conflict between marriage and work

Our hard materialism puts almost as much pressure on the family as the permissive society does. It is an oddity that the richer we become, the more pressure there seems to be for a two-income family. It used to be normal for a woman to stay at home while the children were small; now it is normal for them to go back to work almost as soon as their child is weaned. And, at present, as there is more demand for work for which women are qualified, so there is less for men. Some of this is due to the increase in the number of women with qualifications and the drop in the number of jobs like coalmining, which depend on physical strength; but there is also a feeling that to bring up a child is not as important as it is to hold down a skilled or professional job.

If more employers ran crèches for small children it would be a great deal easier to reconcile work with motherhood; and it would seem good economic sense for them to keep the continuity of skilled and professional workers which a crèche would give. Trading estates could combine to run crèches where the companies were too small, and in city centres it should not be hard to run a combined crèche.

It is also hard for women who have taken six or seven years off to get back into the discipline of work and to catch up with the technical changes since they left. I used to get European funds for a splendid organisation, the Cambridge Women's Resources Centre, which helped women to find their feet and learn new skills before going back to work. We could do with more projects like that.

But if there are no available crèches, if hiring a nanny would be too expensive and if the maternity leave is short, then a baby has only one mother and, for the time being, it needs her, unless in a family's particular circumstances it is more appropriate for

the father to be the main child carer. However, apart from brief
paternity leave when their children are born, most fathers have
to go out to work and, so far, employers are more flexible in
their arrangements with mothers than with fathers.

I do not think it is any part of Christian teaching to say that
a woman's place is, as the Germans used to say, *Kinder, Kirche,
Küche* (children, church and kitchen). In traditional agricultural
societies, the women worked with the men in the fields, taking
their babies with them. In the last chapter of the book of Proverbs,
the 'wife of noble character',

> selects wools and flax and works with eager hands . . . she
> considers a field and buys it; out of her earnings she plants a
> vineyard . . . she sees that her trading is profitable . . . holds
> the distaff and grasps the spindle with her fingers. She opens
> her arms to the poor and extends her hands to the needy . . .
> she makes linen garments and sells them, and supplies the
> merchants with sashes . . . She watches over the affairs of
> her household and does not eat the bread of idleness.

At the end of his letter to the Romans, the apostle Paul asks them
to receive 'our sister Phoebe, a servant of the church in Cenchreae'
and to 'give her any help she may need from you, for she has been a
great help to many people, including me'. He also sends greetings to
Priscilla and Aquila, 'my fellow-workers . . . all the churches of the
Gentiles are grateful to them. Greet also the church that meets in
their house.' And he sends greetings to half a dozen other women
who have been involved in the work of the churches.

So it is clear that the Christian model of marriage is one in
which there is room for a woman to use her talents to the full and
not, as in some religions, to be kept out of sight in a back room or
to have to share her home with other of her husband's wives.

Husbands

Husbands can be even more gripped by materialism than their
wives. We are not yet a society in which the only measure of a
man's worth is his bank balance; but we are fast going that way.

I once managed a large business in which, when I arrived, I found that by far the most intractable decision was the pecking order in company cars. It took such time and heat that I quickly passed it on to a committee and that at least diffused the heat.

Perhaps the most important joint decision between husband and wife is the kind of job a husband should take. Some professions, such as the armed forces, demand separation and wives know what they can expect when they marry. And there are professions which demand very hard work at a junior level. But, where there is a choice, late hours, work all weekend and extended overseas trips should be banned! And Christians above all should avoid the equivalent of the golf widow: the elder or minister who is so busy with church business that he neglects his family. That is no example to set.

A Christian balance

Christian marriage gives a framework in which a partnership of two can come to agreement on decisions which affect them both. With one hand it gives the husband the decisive vote, 'The husband is head of the wife as Christ is the head of the church, his body.' But his authority is limited, because he has to behave to her as Christ would to the church, so in making his casting vote, he must be self-sacrificing and love his wife 'as Christ loved the church and gave himself up for her . . . husbands ought to love their wives as their own bodies . . . each one of you also must love his wife as he loves himself, and the wife must respect her husband' (Eph. 5). And their physical relations must be on equal footing, 'The husband should fulfil his marital duty to his wife, and likewise the wife to her husband. The wife's body does not belong to her alone but also to her husband. In the same way, a husband's body does not belong to him alone but also to his wife. Do not deprive each other except by mutual consent' (1 Cor. 7). The Christian view of marriage is centred on this mutual obligation, not on the dominance of one partner over the other.

It is hard to see a better way of keeping together through all the hazards of life than this partnership at the heart of the family. It does not treat the wife as one of a number of chattels; it does not put her in the charge of her mother-in-law; it does not rely on sending for the police to break up the argument or by one side or the other having to walk out and leave their children behind. It can be supported by those to whom either spouse might look for help and advice – the wider family or the church – and, if church practice and advice wanders, the authority of the apostolic teaching can be used to bring them back.

In a world full of folly and temptation, it seems to work. Christian churches are not immune, but, at a time when one marriage in two is breaking up – more if we take those who live together without legal marriages – the number of committed Christians who split up remains very small. Christians have the other bit of glue which makes marriage stick: the duty of forgiveness. We are not to bear grudges, we are to forgive each other as God has forgiven us. We are to remember that we too have faults.

Motherhood and apple-pie

My wife and I went not long ago to the Norman Rockwell Museum in Stockbridge, Massachusetts. Rockwell idealised American life. His most famous painting is of a little old lady and her grandson saying grace in a 'diner' under the awed gaze of a group of rough workers. In the Rockwell paintings the family had its problems, but it was still the centre of life – Pop, Mom and the kids.

That is a long, long way from the America of today. We may not have gone quite so far over the top as the Americans, and Continental Europe has not gone so far as Britain. But even Christians may wonder whether there is a way back. It has become quite common today to hear that a woman and a child have been murdered and that the police are looking for the woman's former husband or lover. The talk of civilised divorce seems a very long way from the reality of murder in the family, the tip of an iceberg of hate and resentment, which results from the break up of marriage, whether legal or common-law.

As the number of divorces soar, the children coming up to the age of marriage are so disillusioned that half the couples now living together prefer to do so without legal marriage. But that gives even less security in the relationship and, to their children, no security at all. We are beginning to breed a generation of unloved and unwanted children, who owe nothing to anyone, loose cannons in an already broken society.

This is not a new experience for the Christian church. If we read Gibbons' *Decline and Fall of the Roman Empire* or the first chapters of the apostle Paul's letter to the Romans, we see a very similar society. The Christian church did not conform. It went its own way and set an example which was followed, while Rome, like many a corrupt city before it, was destroyed. That is not 'motherhood and apple-pie'. It takes courage to stand out against the trend; but we have to do it, for our sakes, for the sake of our children and grandchildren and for the sake of placing a firm rock on which others can find footing in the middle of the swamp.

Chapter Four

Rebuilding the

PILLARS OF THE MORAL ORDER

Theirs not to reason why,
Theirs but to do and die.

Today we do not accept that logic. We do want to know the reason why. Law should not be irrational, it must rest on a foundation of reason. So it must have a moral basis. Even in a primitive society, there has to be some creed. It may be superstitious and irrational, but it gives a reason why people should hold to their customs. In communism it was the class struggle; in national socialism the racial struggle; and these justified all the harshness of the regimes. But free societies, which ask questions, need more reasoned answers.

If we Christians believe that our moral order is the best foundation for our country's social order, then we have to make the case for it. We let that case go by default if we try to trim to the mood of society. Church leaders must not adjust the Christian moral law to keep on the right side of changeable public opinion.

Church leaders sell the pass

Church leaders allowed the unprovable metaphysical theory of Darwinism to pass as part of the scientific method; people came to believe that science had proved that there was no Creator to whom we owed our being. Theological colleges accepted the German higher criticism which started from the assumption that the Bible was the word of men and not of God and on that assumption, not surprisingly, decided that it contradicted itself and was an unreliable guide. That left them free to invent their own faith and label it as Christianity. But to ordinary people it simply signalled that church leaders no longer believed in Christianity.

Having given up their basic authority to say why we should stick to a Christian moral law, they could do little to brake the decline in the social and moral order – the progroms, purges, holocaust and war of the horrendous first half of the twentieth century. And because they were part of the governing establishment which had allowed the horror, they soon faded out as an intellectual influence and left a vacuum which has been filled with false prophets.

Modernism

The first false prophet was modernism, which taught that science had the answer to everything. Since the scientific method was founded on a Christian understanding of nature, science developed apace; infant mortality decreased and people lived longer. Life became easier for millions and there was hope of economic development for millions more. To begin with, the man in the white coat was the hope of the future.

World War I was a setback, but there was the League of Nations and a determination that such a war would never happen again. But first the Communists and then the Nazis walked into the moral vacuum. Finally the scientists invented the weapon of mass destruction, and after Hiroshima and Nagasaki people began to be frightened of the power of the man in the white coat, who was able to kill millions in a split second and was not under any moral control.

The anorak brigade

The man in the white coat was opposed by the men and women in anoraks, protesting against the damage that uncontrolled science was doing to the natural world. The Aldermaston marches repudiated nuclear weapons. The men and women in anoraks asked politicians awkward questions about whether they would ever press the nuclear button. It was pointed out that the acronym for the Mutual Assured Destruction policy of NATO was MAD. Hard questions were asked about the effect of nuclear power stations on surrounding population and finally nuclear power was driven to the margins. There were Christians who headed the Campaign for Nuclear Disarmament. Others, like the Rev. John Stott and Archbishop Runcie, did not commit themselves to unilateral nuclear disarmament, but were quite clear that a strategy which rested on the threat to take innocent life on a massive scale must be wrong. It was for politicians to find ways of disarmament on both sides, regardless of the non-nuclear cost of defending freedom.

The anorak brigade took up with enthusiasm the cause of the environment and formed a political party, the Greens, who began to influence the political debate. They argued that science was destroying the ecological balance, that whole species were in danger. Christians, who had believed all along that the Creator had given us a balanced ecology and that we held the world of nature in trust for future generations, could agree with all of this. Christians were among those who joined the World Wide Fund for Nature and were among the soaring numbers joining the Royal Society for the Protection of Birds.

But many other people in anoraks were feeling for their own moral basis, which was quite different from that of the Christians. They began to talk about the goddess Gaia and it was not long before some of them had found the ancient pagan worship of nature. Druids reappeared and, at the solstice, Stonehenge became once more a place of worship. There was an annual festival at Glastonbury and a growing New Age cult and shops sprang up, selling cultic symbols.

Post-modernism

Among the intellectuals, modernism was repudiated and what has been called 'post-modernism' took its place. Where modernism looked for hard facts, post-modernism decided that we could be sure of nothing. It is not so much a belief as an insistence that there can be no absolute belief. Everything is relative. Even the contents of a book are uncertain; everyone is free to read into them what they see themselves. Not only was certainty out, but active deconstruction was in. There were no longer any pillars to society. Everyone could believe what they liked. The only truth was that there was no truth.

This was the intellectual background to the permissive society. All had to be free to decide for themselves. It was irrelevant to ask 'why?' It was, of course, a step in faith; so much was it deemed self-evident that there was very little debate. The age-old Christian moral order had to move over and allow everyone to do what they wanted. We were back in the moral chaos so graphically described towards the end of the book of Judges which repeats the refrain, 'Everyone did as he saw fit.'

Thirty years on we have seen the results in Britain so perhaps it is time to look again at the Christian moral order, which served us so well for so long.

The Christian moral order – personal experience

The Christian answer to the question 'why?' is not simply that we believe in the God revealed in the Bible, but that we have put our belief to the test and have found it valid. We find that what we read in the Bible about human nature is truer to life than anything we read elsewhere. We discover that if we ask God to forgive us, we are given a sense of peace which we never had before. We find that a sharpened conscience makes us want to do what we are told to do and miserable when we do the opposite.

But, above all, we find that the lifelong dialogue of reading God's word and praying to him is real. There is an active response to prayer. Often we are given what we ask for – and to begin with we are always slightly surprised – and when we do not receive a positive answer, we are made, though not always at once, to know the reason why. Although, in one sense, the relationship is spiritual, in another it is intensely practical and, over the years, we know that we are dealing with a person, wiser by far than we are, but also gentle and loving and infinitely patient.

And, as time goes on, we read of the same experience of people of God down the ages. We know exactly what David is talking about in his psalms; we have a fellow-feeling with the apostle Paul and with the stories, spread over two thousand years, of those who believe what we believe and have also found it to be true; true to the Bible, true to life outside the church and true to the life of fellow Christians of every age, race and nation.

We also find that, despite all that is said against it, the sense of right and wrong of the people we meet and know who are not Christian corresponds to the Christian moral order. Of course all are protective of their own special weakness; but their view of what is right and wrong in other people is very much the same as ours. It seems to be true that the God we read about has given everyone a conscience, which gives us all the same message. And when people go against their conscience, they feel bad about it. They do not admit that it is conscience, they say, 'I feel bad about myself', or 'I hate myself'. They spend a lot of money going to psychiatrists, but it doesn't seem to mend the hurt.

The Christian moral order – justice

At the centre of the Christian moral order is a strong sense of justice. People have understood that we believe in a God of love and we do. But he is also a God of justice. All through the writings of the Jewish prophets is the strong call for justice for the helpless and oppressed. Isaiah says, 'Your rulers . . . all love bribes and chase after gifts. They do not defend the cause of the fatherless; the widow's case does not come before them' (Isa. 1:23) and '"the plunder from the poor is in your houses. What do you mean by crushing my people and grinding the faces of the poor?" declares the Lord, the Lord Almighty' (Isa. 3:14–15).

Amos is just as outspoken: 'Hear this word, you cows of Bashan on Mount Samaria, you women who oppress the poor and crush the needy and say to your husbands, "Bring us some drinks!"' (Amos 4:1). Christ also called for justice for the oppressed: 'Woe to you, teachers of the law and Pharisees, you hypocrites! . . . You have neglected the more important matters of the law – justice, mercy and faithfulness' (Matt. 23:23).

Justice recognises that there is right and wrong; that right should be rewarded and that wrong must be punished. There can be no moral order in a society in which there is no sense of justice and a refusal to believe in right and wrong. At this point we are totally opposed to the post-modernists and believe that it is a contradiction in terms to hold so dogmatically that there is no dogma.

Economic morality

Justice in the Old Testament is not just left as a vague principle. It is spelt out in some detail. There are regulations for honest weights and measures (Prov. 11:1; 20:10; Micah 6:11) and severe strictures on those lenders who abuse their power over the needy borrower. Usury, however it is defined, was disallowed. If someone was really needy and did not have the money for the seed for the next season's crop, his neighbour should be generous and not charge him a rate of interest which would force him to pay with part of his property. The rich should not be greedy, adding field to field and house to house (Isa. 5:8). And, on the fiftieth year, the year of jubilee (Lev. 25:10), all property, however gained, was to go back to the original family. Family land was inalienable. It was the source of wealth and no family should be forced to part with it for ever.

The way in which these principles work out can seldom be applied directly to industrial society; but since Christ endorsed the law of Moses, the principles certainly apply with full force to Christians as individuals. What they tell us is that our business dealings should be governed by morality rather than the market and that the citizen should not be reduced to servitude by the accidents of the market. The market must serve mankind and not mankind the market.

These principles are also redistributive. They do not say that wealth should cascade down without end to generation after generation, giving a fraction of the population the great majority of the wealth. The Old Testament law of the jubilee laid down that since land, their means of production, was inalienable, then every fifty years it should revert to the family originally entitled.

In modern terms the principle might mean that we may keep what we earn ourselves and to pass it on to our heirs, but that two generations is enough. That used to be the effect of capital transfer taxes on death, when taxes were pitched at a level which did not allow vast estates to descend beyond the grandchildren of those who earned them. Were we to have the same level of tax again and for the same purpose, the proceeds of the tax should not go back into general revenue, but should be reserved for projects which give a stake in society to those without it.

'What is truth?'

Even more important to the integrity of society, both Old and New Testaments teach the importance of honesty. At his trial Christ talked to Pilate about truth and the world-weary Pilate asked, 'What is truth?' (John 18:38). But a society which corrupts the truth is doomed. The worst sin of post-modernism is to identify with Pontius Pilate's cynicism.

The whole of our modern industrial society depends on truth. The validity of scientific research is absolutely vital to the progress of science. Fraudulent claims are not only dangerous to human life, they undermine society's trust in the scientific method which is the basis of our high-tech society. But more common are the temptations to claim for science what has not and sometimes cannot be validated.

Those who make the claims may say in the small print that the proposition will need more work. But the headline in the paper makes readers believe that the work is almost complete; that there are cures just around the corner when no one can really judge how long it might take; that a process is safe when it is not safe; that the origin of life in a primeval soup has been shown to be scientifically possible – even though the chances against are impossibly high and events in time past can never be validated experimentally.

We rely on the validity of science for safe food, safe travel, safe medicine, safe bridges, safe buildings and safe equipment in our homes and at work and if the growing mistrust of science were to get out of hand, our society would be paralysed. Already it sometimes seems that there is little left that is safe to eat or drink. Honesty is a critical need of the industrial society in which we live. Whatever the post-modernists may say, there is truth and there are lies and our lives depend on our being able to tell one from the other.

Commercial honesty

Commercial honesty is as important, for the whole of our complex industrial society depends on trust. Buyers may do a spot-check on what they buy, but if, instead, they had to examine every purchase in detail, business would grind to a halt. A company depends on its buyers to make sure that what it buys is up to specification. If it could not trust its buyers and the owners had to check everything themselves, to make sure there had been no bribery or carelessness, then all business would have to be conducted on a small scale, as, in so many countries, it still is. And international trade, on which we in Britain depend, would dry up.

Finance, too, depends overwhelmingly on honesty. We have to trust our pensions and our savings to the people running huge institutions, whom we have never met. We hope that somewhere, someone is keeping a check on them, But, as institutions get bigger, building societies become banks and banks remove the human face of the local bank manager; finance becomes more international; 'managed funds' distance us from the companies into which our money goes and there are markets in 'derivatives', whatever they may be. We may sometimes wonder whether anyone really knows what goes on.

This feeling is not helped by the scandals.

- the failure of BCCI, an international bank where no one seemed to know what was going on;
- the scandal of the prestigious Lloyds insurance market, where respected and trusted insiders creamed the safest risks for themselves and left the outsiders, who had pledged all their assets, with the worst risks which took many of them to near ruin;
- the Maxwell scandal, where major banks lent their depositors' money to a man whom a public investigation had long

ago labelled as unfit to be in charge of a public company and who proved it by making off with the funds of the company's own pensioners; and

- the failure of Barings, the oldest and most prestigious of the merchant banks, whose directors were evidently unable to control an employee, who took enormous and fatal risks in their name by buying and selling 'futures' – the currency and other market risks which individual companies could not carry themselves.

Those who hold our money know that the financial markets rely on trust and that a general failure of trust would be catastrophic. No bank can pay back all its depositors at once and a major failure of confidence – a crash – can close down the whole system. Regulatory bodies did not seem to be able to deal in time with any of these recent failures, so the system needs far better self-regulation than it has at present.

Today's absentee landlords

All companies, including financial institutions, are meant to be under the control of directors who are appointed by the shareholders. It is probably the two links, between shareholders and directors and between directors and management, which need to be strengthened by the right kind of legislation. After the property boom collapse of 1973/4, when many banks were badly hit, the old Jewish merchant banks – still under the control of Kleinworts, Warburgs and Rothschilds – survived. They not only had long memories, but they were still controlling shareholders and still managed the business. I was at that time managing director of John Laing, which had large property interests. The company was still largely owned and controlled by the Laing family and we, too, did not follow the market and also emerged unscathed.

On the other hand, three people I have known, each distinguished in his own field, had moved over to become chairman of one or other of the great clearing banks only to discover some can of worms for which they were not themselves responsible but which, when it came to light, did their reputation no good at all. The problem seems to be that the boards of the clearing banks have been used as honorary positions for those who represent the banks' largest customers, rather than those who know anything about banking or who are active and independent representatives of the shareholders.

No good case has been made for the change in status of the traditional building societies who now want to become banks – a business in which they have no obvious expertise. If the building society bribes its major depositors with an offer of free shares when the deal goes through, rather than with good reasons why their money would be safer or their interest higher, then there must be some doubt as to whether a good reason exists.

When the financial institutions are themselves shareholders, they do not seem unduly concerned to exercise their rights. The general rule is that if they do not like the way a company is going, they do not try to change it; rather they sell their shares to those who know less than they do and seem more interested in the short-term share value than in the long-term management of the company – the short-termism of which so many complain. So a tightening-up of the links between shareholders, directors and management seems right not only for financial institutions, but also for all shareholders.

The moral issue is not only that there should be transparency in all financial transactions and in relations between owners and managers, but also that ownership carries responsibilities. We should not allow size and complexity to confuse a responsibility which was clear when workers knew who their bosses were and their behaviour for good or ill was there for all to see.

Honesty in politics

Party politics also pollute the well of truth. There comes a time when the disillusion is so great that it affects not just the leaders who lie, but the whole of the political process. I do not believe that leaders start out with the intention of misleading. But honourable men and women, who go into politics for the highest of motives, discover that what they say affects not just themselves but all in their parliamentary party who want to achieve political power.

When the troops behind are baying for blood, it is hard to resist. So the truth is buried under a mountain of half-truth, innuendo and diversion.

In part, this is the result of the two-party system. When you are in government, everything you do is right and justifiable. When you are in opposition, everything the government does is wrong and outrageous. The listening public know that this cannot possibly be true and come to regard the whole parliamentary debate as a useless sham. So damage is done not just to the truth, but to the democratic process. When a constitution requires a government to command a majority of the popular vote so that more than one party is involved, the argument has to be addressed to the real issues; because action depends on a wider consensus than can be found in one party alone and power comes from the centre and not from the extremes.

Truth also has a better chance if there is a separation of powers; if parliament sees its main function as a check on the executive, its main power in informed cross-examination of those holding power. If a parliamentary committee always has a majority of members from the government party, then its comments will always be muted; but if there is a real separation of powers, then the cross-examination should discover the truth.

But in our two-party system – when the whips hold the gates to power in the party and the party holds the gates to power in the country – whole issues are buried wherever the official opposition decides that, if they raised their voices, they could lose an impending election. So, though we are a democracy, the electorate are given no say in key issues. A different kind of parliament – with a wider range of parties and more independence on the part of the members – could hammer out a cross-party line on major issues and bring the public into the debate before they finally made up their minds.

Truth in the media

Truth is also dependent on high standards of conduct in press, radio and TV, commonly known as the 'fourth estate' of the realm. A free and unbiased press is absolutely essential to a soundly working democracy. The press has never been perfect, for if a newspaper did not reflect some of the bias and prejudice of its readers, no one would buy it. But there is a wide difference today between the broadsheets – which do try to report the news – and the tabloids which, in fierce competition with each other and with TV, are mainly entertainment. There is also a noticeable difference between the foreign-owned national broadsheets on the one hand and the few independent national broadsheets and the provincial press on the other.

The big foreign cartels have their own commercial agenda and a heavy bias to news and comment which supports it, omitting entirely news and comment which does not. That seems to involve an agenda aimed to rubbish our European neighbours and to stir up English nationalism, which does immense harm to our relations with those who are our neighbours and want to be our friends.

But the greatest distortion comes from the need of television producers to reduce news to soundbites and gripping pictures. This cuts out a great deal which is far more important than the pieces which are shown, and unbalances what we do see. It devalues parliamentary debate and gives the initiative to the party in power. It devalues local politics and reinforces the centralisation of political power in London. And, because government can use TV to reach over the heads of elected politicians, it gives a determined prime minister the presidential power of setting the agenda and of swamping out what is inconvenient with a flood of diverting material which, coming from the centre of political power, the media cannot ignore.

There is nothing more exasperating for a footslogging politician than to knock on doors and find minds locked in the belief that if something has not appeared on the telly, it cannot be important or, even worse, if it has appeared, then the version on the telly is a fact of life!

Journalists and TV producers argue that they are simply giving a mirror image of society. If society does not like what it sees in the mirror, it has only itself to blame. There is a lot in this argument. If people do not like what they see or read, they will switch off or buy another paper. But there is a very real power there too. TV not only puts out the news; it is itself part of the scene it has to describe. Those who appear regularly on the small box are national personalities and people want to know their opinions. Go to the biographical section of a bookshop. It is the TV personalities who are most popular. They are the popularly appointed modern prophets. And though those in charge of TV have to keep a balance on programmes, it is they who set the agenda, who decide what is included and what is cut out of the public debate. They are therefore under enormous pressure from vested interests, including political parties. So we rely heavily on their honesty and integrity.

Maybe just as important, it is almost impossible for the private citizen to correct damaging personal misinformation. The very poor may get state aid to sue for libel and the rich may be able to afford it; but most people cannot afford to sue a national newspaper.

I once asked the editor of the *New Statesman* to correct a piece which listed my company as one of the absentee owners of highland deer forests who kept them for shooting parties and prevented local people from earning a living. He printed my letter, which said that, apart from MacBrayne's Boats, we were in fact the biggest employers north of the highland line and ran at a substantial loss the deer forests, which we had bought only for their water rights which we needed for the hydroelectric power for our aluminium smelters. The *Financial Times* did not read the letter and printed a piece similar to that in the *New Statesman*. I again persuaded the editor to print a correction in a prominent place. Then *Panorama*, having read neither the *NS* nor the *FT* corrections, sent a TV team to our estates to find and interview someone who would say that we had prevented them from earning a living. My chairman had to threaten a libel action before they ran an apology at the beginning of the next week's programme. If a large company can have difficulties, pity the private citizens who do not have the resources to threaten libel actions.

Reporters tend to run in packs. TV pick up on a story which has already appeared in the press. They do not feel comfortable in going out on a limb, because their editor will ask why they alone have the right angle, when all other papers have come to a different conclusion.

But, with all their faults, the media are now one of the indispensable pillars of a free society. They may not be perfect;

but those of us who have had to deal with societies which are not free know the difference which freedom of information makes. A minister of trade from a great Communist country once told a parliamentary committee that 'all the people are behind the government's new trade policy'. But how could she know? The press would have got its line from the government. Her officials would not have dared to contradict her. And any citizen asked by an official whether they supported the new policy would, no doubt, have nodded vigorously. No one dared tell President Kim Il-sung that the North Korean economy was bankrupt. President Ceausescu of Romania did not know that he had lost popular support until the crowd outside the palace howled him down.

There are powerful interests who use every argument they can to prevent their exposure to the truth. So they use every abuse of the power of the press to undermine it. If the media loses the battle, it will be because the public are persuaded that their abuse of power has made it a danger to the individual rather than their protector. So it is in all our interests that the press should police itself and restrain its excesses.

No one who has been in British public life can doubt the salutary effect of the freedom of the press. It is hard to get away with lies for very long. Scandals are uncovered, cover-ups laid bare, pomposity punctured, evasions exposed as the fresh breeze of truth blows away the fog.

The dignity of the individual

The Christian faith is a far more effective protection of the individual and of democracy than any theory of human rights. Christians believe that men and women are made in the image of God (Gen. 1:26–27; 9:6); that we are not descended by accident from primeval slime; that the extraordinary body which we inhabit – with its self-healing powers, its ability to communicate and its extraordinary inventiveness – cannot be a cosmic accident, but was designed for a purpose. We also believe that the human being is above the animals and not just another, more intelligent beast. And, above all, we believe that we are made to live in company with the God who made us for himself.

If, instead, society believes that humans were a cosmic accident, then people will value their fellow beings accordingly: we will see women as sex objects and believe that those of other races or classes are inferior. If those who profess to be Christians allow themselves to be influenced by their culture, like the slave-owners of the southern states of America, then a crusade has to be launched to right the wrong. And when churches had special seats for the rich, they were contradicting a specific command in the letter of James to the churches. Until the 1960s our cartoonists, while exaggerating their characters, made them more than human; but from the sixties on, most cartoons dehumanise their characters. Today cartoons are hardly recognisable as human beings and pornography, male now as well as female, makes the person no more than an object of lust and violence. It is small wonder that there has been such a huge increase in crimes of violence against the person.

For the Christian, all human beings – however poor, however incapacitated, however simple – are eternal beings, accountable to our divine Maker for all we do, say and think; beings of such infinite worth that God the Son took on human form to die for us, so that, despite all our rebellion against him, we could be reconciled to God. Those beliefs about the dignity of our fellow men and women are at the core of the Christian moral order. We are told to love God above all, and if we love the Father, we should love his children, who are our neighbours, as ourselves. It is the evidence of this loving care that does more for the Christian faith than all intellectual argument. People respond to love when they are deaf to argument.

This love for our neighbour knows no barrier of race or class. When Christ was asked, 'Who is my neighbour?' he told the story of the Good Samaritan. A priest and a Levite had passed the wounded man on the Jericho road and it was a Samaritan who came to his aid, cleaned and bound his wounds, took him to an inn and paid the innkeeper to look after him. The message to Christ's Jewish audience was clear. Our neighbour is whoever is in need and depends on us for help, even if they are from another race and religion. The Jews would not even speak to Samaritans since they despised them for both their race and religion, but, in Christ's parable, the Samaritan helped the wounded Jew.

Violence

If it is wrong to neglect our neighbour, for whom the Son of God died, violence against someone made in the image of God is a far worse crime than robbery. And to take away the life which God has given is the worst of all crimes against mankind. Since the fifties the rate of murder in our country has multiplied by five, the rate of violent crime by twelve and the rate of violent crime by young people has multiplied by fifteen. In towns and cities streets are no longer considered safe and the police are no longer able to deliver the criminal to justice.

The balance of terror is now on the side of the criminal. If they take hostages and threaten to shoot them, the police must reckon that the hostages' lives are at risk. But the police cannot make a similar threat against the terrorists to protect the hostages. So, not only are five times as many innocent people killed, but innocent hostages, including children, are now put at risk. There is now little added risk in killing a witness to a crime, since the added sentence, if a violent attack ends in death, is only a matter of degree; so, within a generation, criminals carry guns and police have had to respond in kind.

Once power slips from the hands of the police, guns and the gangs which hold them take over power. I visited a new housing site at Carlisle Circus in Belfast in the early seventies. The site agent had just had a visit from a loyalist paramilitary who told him, at the point of a gun, that he had to have the nationalist tiling subcontractor off the site at once. The agent told me, 'When you look down the wrong end of a gun, you know that if you make a wrong decision, it will be your last.' Twenty years later my wife and I were visiting a church outreach in the St George's district of Bristol, the centre of the local drug trade. A few weeks before that, an armed gang, the 'Yardies', had come down from London and made the local drug dealers lie face down on the street while they removed all the drugs and all the cash, got in their cars and went back along the M4 to London, no one stopping them. We are not far from gun law.

In the early seventies, when pornography was first legalised, I served as treasurer to the Longford Commission, which looked at its likely effect. At the time we were able to do very little, for the tide was flowing strongly in favour of 'freedom'. But twenty years later we can see the effect, not only of the trade which degrades women, but of the pornography of violence, not now confined to the literature of sex, but in the much more vivid videos of both sex and violence. In weak and vacant minds, the images lead on to an attitude which makes the deeds seem to be a natural part of life instead of the horrible perversion that it is. Children are mown down in a school in Dunblane and a headmaster is knifed to death by a teenage gang leader when trying to protect a pupil at the school gate.

A society without a moral order to underpin its institutions is on its way to disintegration. It is easy enough to remove long-founded beliefs by proclaiming freedom from moral restraint. To rebuild a voluntary moral system is far harder. The first step is to admit failure and to recognise the need for a cohesive and compelling set of beliefs which will help us to rebuild our relationships with each other. It is hard to see what can improve on the known, tried and tested beliefs of the Christian faith.

THE ECONOMIC ORDER

Chapter Five

NAKED GREED

Let us eat, drink and be merry, for tomorrow we die!

Shop-floor greed weakened the unions

When I first went into public life in 1964, trades unions – formed to use the bargaining power of the strong to help the weak – covered nearly half of the country's workforce. Unemployment varied between a quarter of a million in good times and half a million in bad times. Today the unions are far weaker; unemployment varies between two million in good times and over three million in bad times – and many of those in work are now on insecure short-term contracts.

The first indication of the weakening of trades union members' loyalty to their ideals came in 1969, when I was director general of the National Economic Development Council. I warned the council, composed of senior cabinet ministers, trades union leaders and industrialists, that, for the first time, wage awards were rising despite rising unemployment. The trades union leaders found it hard to believe, because they knew that they had not authorised the rate of increase which I was reporting. The answer was that those who had the strongest bargaining power – those in the private sector whose strikes could hold companies to ransom – were using their bargaining power to help themselves and not to help their fellow workers.

From then on, the union leaders had to do what they could to help those without shop-floor power, including the huge public sector, to catch up. The resulting wage–price spiral led to the biggest inflation in the history of our country and cut the value of the pound by nine-tenths over thirty years. It led to huge public sector strikes, one of which, the miners' strike of 1973–4, brought about the fall of the Conservative government and another of which, the 'winter of discontent' in 1978–9, led to the collapse of support for the Labour government which succeeded it.

Vulnerable employers struck back. The most vulnerable, the national daily newspapers, automated their entire process, dispensing with hot metal and going over to papers typeset by journalists. The next most vulnerable, the car industry, went to the Japanese model and automated the production line, buying in everything they could from subcontractors and double-sourcing in case of strikes against a supplier. Since then there has been a huge loss of jobs in manufacturing industry and a great increase of competitive pressure on subcontractors.

But perhaps the biggest blow was the frank abandonment by the new 1979 Thatcher government of the postwar policy of full employment. Mrs Thatcher took advantage of the new oil boom to allow the pound to rise by 20 per cent, cutting the price of competitive imports and raising the cost of our own exports. It cut our share of world trade in manufacturing by over 20 per cent and we lost our long-time surplus in manufacturing trade, which we have never since recovered. It raised the level of unemployment to an incredible three and a half million, but the lower cost of imports allowed her to raise real incomes for those still in jobs and she was twice re-elected by voters, which made practical politicians believe that idealism was out and that money in the pocket was all that counted.

She was also determined not to allow the miners to do to her what they did to her predecessor. The government started to import coal, to close pits, and to build up a strategic stockpile, so that they could stand a long strike. With appalling incompetence Scargill, the miners' leader, called a strike in the middle of the summer when demand was lowest and stocks were highest and did not ballot his members for their approval. He lost and the closure of the pits proceeded apace, leaving whole towns to rot.

The trades unions recognised what was known euphemistically

as the 'new reality': that the haves did not care as much for the have-nots as they did for their own pockets; but that did not stop them from losing four million members, from a peak of eleven million, down to seven million. The Labour Party also recognised the 'new reality', but that did not prevent their new leader from losing a third and a fourth election, while Tony Blair, the third leader since Jim Callaghan was prime minister, became reluctant to get too far from the policies which elected four Conservative governments in a row.

Greed in the boardroom

Those who work on the shop floor may be forgiven for getting what they can in a hard world. But greed by those who do not really need it is less forgivable. In the seventies, when I was chairman and later vice president of the British Institute of Management, I used to argue with a Labour government against the disincentive effect of their level of personal taxes. They rose in steep progression to 83 per cent on earned income and to 98 per cent on dividends. I said that those in business, whether manager or entrepreneur, ran risks which did not exist in the public service and if they were not allowed a risk premium, they would not take the risks.

But, from the 1980s on, we have gone to the other extreme. Not only have direct taxes on higher incomes been drastically reduced, but those who find themselves in charge of denationalised monopolies are paying themselves huge salaries and bonuses which are, in most people's view, out of all proportion to the limited commercial risks that they run. And the bonuses and free shares awarded to those who do have risks are far more than enough to keep them comfortable for the rest of a long life if they lose their job and cannot find another.

Greed in the City

I still have a great respect for the City of London and its institutions, where I served my apprenticeship; but it has become too careless of its reputation for handling other people's money on which it depends. It is not entirely to blame. The deregulation of financial markets has introduced fierce competition for business and has tempted sober bankers to take risks which their predecessors would not have touched with the proverbial bargepole. A new generation has forgotten the City's golden rule, 'Don't be too greedy.'

The Maxwell affair should be a lesson. Sir Ronald Leach, a much respected senior partner of one of the City's largest accounting firms, was asked in the seventies to report on Robert Maxwell's conduct of his business. Sir Ronald's public report said that he was not a suitable person to be in charge of other people's money, which confirmed the view of those who knew something about him. Yet, despite this public warning, he was able to borrow enough money in the City to buy control of the *Daily Mirror* and so to mismanage it that he raided its pension fund in an attempt to keep the company solvent, before he finally gave up and was lost overboard.

There have been hard words with the insurance companies who ended up with the pension fund assets and, for the reputation of the City, the pensioners will no doubt get most of their money back. But the foundation of the pension fund and banking business is that our money can be safe with strangers and there have been too many of these scrapes: Lloyds of London, Barings and, the latest, Morgan Grenfell, which had to be bailed out by its new German owners. How long will the reputation of the City survive the sight of senior executives creaming off profits for themselves at the expense of those who have trusted them?

Deregulation of the financial markets led directly to the 'Barber boom' of the early seventies and to the 'Lawson boom' of the eighties, each of which had its inevitable slump, ending with those who could look after themselves much richer and those who could not much poorer – or bankrupt. In both booms the big banks poured money in and, when the slump came, wanted their money back at once. After the 'Lawson boom' many small businesses simply could not find the money quickly enough and house repossessions went up to record levels. Those of us who have had to represent constituents will always remember the innocent losers.

The contrast could hardly be greater between the City in which I served my time and the City as it is today. The financial reputation of the City of London was built on trust, that your life savings could be trusted to people whom you did not know. Its trade was also built on trust between merchants, trust that deals would be fair and reasonable and that both sides would keep to their commitments. Not any longer.

It hit me first in the early seventies when a merchant bank of hitherto high repute offered a 'legal' method of turning a government subsidy for the shipping industry into a subsidy for a construction company. We turned it down and never went back to them. Today the process of doing government out of its legitimate revenues is big business, made easier by the huge expansion in off-shore tax havens.

I was told by a senior Price Waterhouse manager who was about at the time that when, in the thirties crash, the speculator Hattray went to the Price Waterhouse partner to explain his position, the partner listened carefully and then said simply, 'Here is a telephone, and that is the number of the Director of Public Prosecutions.' Today's Hattrays no doubt find it possible to go elsewhere and find the money to see them through.

Short-term profits squeeze out long-term investment

The City has also something to answer for in the wave after wave of hostile takeover bids, where the ownership of companies employing thousands was treated as no more than a hand in a game of cards for very high stakes. Legally directors are responsible to shareholders and not to workers; but good private ownership believed that power carried responsibilities. Those working in private companies knew who they worked for and who was responsible if they were treated harshly. When private companies went public the former ownership usually stayed on, but when the hostile takeovers replaced it, the owners became anonymous. Workers were faced with absentee landlords and the business where they earned their living became just like another thousand Irish acres to be bought or sold.

Takeovers were big business for those in the City who handled them and they made fortunes for those who sold out; but it was not clear that they served any economic purpose. In the late sixties, when I was director general of the NEDC, we looked into the economic case for mergers and found that nine-tenths were defensive, to increase the market value of the merged company sufficiently to put it beyond the reach of a hostile bid. Of the remainder, academic studies seemed unable to find any economic improvement, except that a larger share of the market helped curtail competition.

As any soldier will tell us, morale is vital to performance. But the first condition of high morale is trust between those who have to make decisions and those who have to carry them out. Constant changing of a management team can only destroy trust.

I had a first-hand account of a new post-merger manager's encounter with the workers in a plant in South Wales. He told them of all the improvements in efficiency he was going to make and an old worker responded, 'You're the fifth to come down here and tell us something like that. None of them lasted and nor will you.' Nor did he. A company chairman asked me once why he could not get the trust of the workers. I told him that it was because chairmen of that company normally stayed in the job for only two years. How could they put their trust in someone who would shortly disappear?

The most recent result of absentee landlordism is the pressure on companies for short-term results. Let us just take a case study, which, though well disguised, has the merits of being based on real life. A large company is rich with the profits of a product which has only a few years more before technical changes will make it obsolete and all the company's customers will be free to choose alternatives. The company has the great advantage of a huge customer base and of customer inertia. It knows much more about the technical side of the business than most outsiders and its new product will have far greater technical credibility than almost any other product on offer. Technically its new product can easily be adapted to cover products now offered by other industries, so there is great scope for expansion. But the new product, though its feasibility is proven, will still need substantial investment before it can go into production.

The board chairman has made his reputation in the financial market by giving sharp increases of year-on-year profits through cost-cutting. His bonuses and those of the immediate top management are geared to the increase of these year-on-year profits and most of them aim to retire within the next five years. It is against their own personal financial interests to have any major investment in the next five years which will depress the earnings per share. The majority of the outside directors are chairman appointees. He sits on their boards and they on his, so backing the chairman is in the joint interest of all concerned. The top staff are also on bonuses geared to short-term earnings, which provides a strong incentive to keep quiet and back the chairman's will.

The chairman does not mount outright opposition to new investment. The line management are asked to produce proposals and that takes about a year. The proposals are then sent back with a request for a wide range of alternatives and that is likely to take another year. Meanwhile the drumbeat from company headquarters is that the markets will only be satisfied with the steady increases in profits which they have constantly enjoyed (but which is incompatible with the heavy investment needed). Market analysts, though aware of the company's long-term needs, are content with what the chairman tells them since they have sold the company to clients as a steady earnings stock and do not want to change the story. As the point of no return approaches – invisible to shareholders and workforce – the bright young managers see the future of the company slipping and begin to look for other jobs.

This is not a unique story. It is all too typical. British and American capital markets suffer from lack of identification of interests of the shareholders with long-term interests of the companies they own. It is a remarkably short-sighted policy and very damaging to the interests of the pension funds who hold the shares against their own long-term liabilities and are not best served by short-termism.

The continental tradition encourages far greater involvement of their shareholders in the companies they own. Relations with employees are far easier when they know that the management, on whom they rely to keep their side of the bargain, will not be removed overnight by a financial coup.

We still have this close cooperation in large private companies and it is essential to taking of critical decisions involving major changes. When I was managing director of John Laing, the owners – in the shape of the chairman and deputy chairman – were just along the corridor. When we wanted to switch from the suicidal competition for motorway contracts to the building of North Sea production platforms, we knew that we had their backing. When we decided not to follow the other property developers in the 1973 boom, we knew that they approved. You cannot discuss proposals with a market, but you can with shareholders or their representatives.

Merger mania

That was very different from my earlier experience in the mid-fifties, when I was chief executive of Costain and we found an unknown buyer whose holding was approaching 18 per cent of the company's capital and looked likely to make a hostile bid. We didn't argue. We devoted our whole attention to giving the market what it wanted: revaluation of properties; buying a partner out and including the full profits of the new subsidiary; forecasting what were fortunately much better group profits; and, above all, paying out a much higher proportion of profits in dividend. None of this made the slightest difference to the real performance of the business, but the share price soared, making a bid too expensive and the speculators sold out and took their profit.

Bidders are not always so fortunate. Twenty-five years later, when I was on the board of Mallinson Denny, one of Britain's three major timber companies, we had a bid from Brooke Bond Tea, who knew nothing about timber. We explained that the current share value reflected a peak in the price of timber and that this was likely to drop steeply in the near future. They made their offer regardless. The timber price dropped and the company's profits with it. This affected the Brooke Bond profits and weakened their shares, making them vulnerable to a successful bid by Unilever, so the workers in our King's Lynn sawmills were in the remote hands of the troika who ran the great food giant. Then Terence Mallinson put together finance for a buy-out from Unilever and Mallinson's went back to square one. I'm told that the Stock Exchange call that process 'churning' and of course it is very good for brokers' commissions.

The economic excuse for hostile takeovers is that if management do not keep on their toes and make the best use of their assets and opportunities, then they will be taken over by someone who will do the job better. I was given the job of managing the British Aluminium Company in 1960 after the biggest hostile takeover bid the City had ever seen, when the great City merchant banks were divided between two camps, each supporting the opposing bids. Those who talk about the benefits of takeovers should try to put together a management team of the old and the new and see how it works out.

It required the steel and wisdom of a unique chairman, Edwin Plowden, to make managements from three quite different backgrounds work together. The change in sales management alone forfeited customer loyalty and lost vital market share. The shares, despite all the City expertise, were bought at the peak of the aluminium price, which dropped smartly immediately afterwards and, during the four years I was there, the market was in chronic surplus with severe international competition. After my time the successful bidders sold out one after the other and I doubt whether they made a profit.

The old management had made mistakes, but it contained some extremely experienced people. Had the company had the continental-type close relationship with the principal owners, the company management would have had to answer awkward questions and would have avoided their main mistakes. Although this is not infallible, it seems to me to be a much more rational way of conducting relationships between owners and management. But, most important, it fulfils the moral obligation that those with power should accept the responsibility which goes with it.

So my long considered view is that 'merger mania' is a result of greed and not of a healthful exercise of an informed market which is needed to improve management and make the best use of resources. Somehow the divorce of power from responsibility must be reversed.

Bribery and corruption

In most countries bribery and corruption are endemic. The outstanding exceptions are the countries where Christian influence has been strongest and where, in the last three hundred years, corruption was gradually curbed and the civil service, the judges, the police and politicians could be relied on not to accept bribes. Within public companies the management could rely on their staff and did not have to worry that the advice they received on the award of contracts, or on the materials and plant which they bought, might be tainted by corruption.

But corruption is starting to creep back. The pornographers of Soho paid for police protection in the late sixties and several high-ranking police officers were caught and sentenced. Also in the late sixties the well-known Kray gang, operating in East London, avoided arrest and it seemed that, until their notoriety spread, they must have paid the metropolitan police to leave them alone. Since then gangs have spread and more policemen have been arrested for taking bribes; a situation not out of control, but extremely worrying.

Corruption is also starting to creep into politics. A large number of MPs are now employed by public relations firms to 'advise' them on legislation which affects their clients. It has been necessary to tighten the rules on public disclosure. But there is still an unpleasant and worrying odour of sleaze.

In the late seventies, when I was chairman of our main export promotion body, the British Overseas Trade Board, our exporters began to be worried about the increasing demands from foreign governments for huge bribes. It was also a major point of discussion at the annual European Management Forum in Davos. The sessions were discreetly labelled 'business ethics', but the overwhelming worry was demands for bribes. Business would say nothing in public and governments, mindful of diplomacy, professed to know nothing; but since these demands came from a third of our export markets, it seemed to be wrong for me to say nothing and I soon became the media's only known expert on bribery and corruption!

We had only to compare the economies of the countries where bribery was rampant with the industrial democracies where it had been held at bay to know that, if it seeped back into our own countries in any strength, it would undermine our whole economic structure. One contractor, tempted to agree to one of their managers making a major bribe, soon found that their own local staff were being offered bribes by those bidding for the local subcontracts. It was a salutary lesson. In a heavily interdependent industrial economy we depend on the integrity of the staff of a company and its inspectors, who make sure that the chemicals, pharmaceuticals, aircraft alloys, brake linings, structural steel and fast food ingredients are up to specification. It is vital that there has been no bribery to certify products not up to specification and not so safe.

Once trust is lost, the company is ruined. And once bribery spreads on any scale, the country is ruined. Trade would grind down and would be conducted mainly between the small-scale enterprises, as it is today in those countries where bribery is rampant and where business has to be conducted between people who trust no one outside their friends and family. The income of the industrial democracies, where honesty is still the best policy, is five to ten times that of the countries where bribery is endemic and would plummet to their level if bribery got a real grip and no one could be trusted.

Bribery is quite properly called 'corruption'. Its effect is to destroy all the structures which are meant to protect the citizen. If the police can be bought, crime pays and people have to pay the mafia for protection. If judges can be bought, there is no justice for the poor. If politicians can be bought, then there is no democracy. If the press can be bought (either individual reporters or editors or a whole chain of media companies), then freedom of speech disappears and religious liberty too.

People say glibly, 'It is the custom of the country.' But it is not the law of any country and those who take bribes only last until the next coup d'état when, if they do not escape to their hard-currency haven, they are dealt with by those who have been waiting to get their own hands in the till. So corruption also leads to political instability, to one dictator after another. And, naturally, the incoming government wants to justify the coup by making an example of the iniquities of its predecessors, so those who have given bribes also find themselves part of the process of rough justice.

The way of the transgressors is hard. A friend of mine, with more courage than most, went to see the military dictator of his country, whom he knew, and told him that he should resign. The dictator

83

agreed that his time was up, but said he could not resign until he had assurances of a waiver from prosecution for his accumulated riches. He never got his waiver; his opponents shot him instead.

This may seem a far cry from Britain. But we only have to go back to the early eighteenth century to Prime Minister Walpole, whose best-known saying was, 'Every man has his price.' If countries lose the Christian heritage which rescued them from corruption, what right have we to believe that we are immune? But if we are not immune, the virus is already working and our whole commercial and industrial system is at risk.

Bribing the electors with their own money

The most dangerous temptation today is the temptation to governments to bribe the electorate with their own money. In the middle of the nineteenth century, bribery of the electorate was outlawed. No longer can candidates stand the public drinks at their expense or offer any kind of benefit in return for a vote. But the bribes offered at Charles Dickens' Eatenswill election are nothing compared with the bribes which governments now offer to the electorate in order to stay in office.

Before the 1959 election, the then prime minister – Harold Macmillan – said, 'Most of our people have never had it so good.' It was the first time a prime minister had pointed to the economic benefit in the run-up to an election and he won. Before the next election we had the 'Maudling boom' which nearly broke the country. It is thought that had we had a 'Jenkins boom', Labour might have won the 1969 election, but we had the 'Barber boom' in 1973, though it peaked too soon. By the election early in 1974 the depression had begun. The government decided to fight on the issue of the miners' strike and lost. In 1979 Jim Callaghan stuck to a 5 per cent flat rate incomes policy and lost to Margaret Thatcher who promised to abolish income restraint and won. In 1983 and 1987 she was able, because of the North Sea oil revenue, to allow unprecedented increase in the real wages of the majority still at work and won an unprecedented two more elections, making three in a row.

By 1992, by spending all the oil surplus and going deep into the red, the majority who were in employment were still much better off than ever before, though at the expense of a minority who were either unemployed, or much worse off. The majority who were better off elected the Conservatives again, and it was clear that the 'new reality' was that it was those in jobs and better off who were now the decisive electoral factor.

As mentioned above, this 'new reality' has pushed the Labour party far further to the right than ever before. Yet it is quite clear to anyone who can add up that government cannot meet the demands for better health, education and police protection and pay the huge bill for the unemployed – let alone curb its rising financial deficit – without raising taxes. But neither government nor opposition dares to put this critical item on the agenda. The 'new unreality' is to have a general election without the great unmentionable, which should be the central issue.

Not so long ago, as we have seen, the basic rate of tax was 33 per cent, with tax on higher earned incomes rising steeply to 83 per cent and a supplement of 15 per cent for unearned income, making an absurdly high top marginal rate of 98 per cent. But now we have gone so far in the opposite direction that we want to take away from government any flexibility in raising taxes even if that is what is needed to get the unemployed back to work again and relieve ourselves of the enormous cost of paying over two million people to do nothing. The only result will be an even bigger tax bill or a return to high inflation, which is the cruellest tax of all, because it is a tax on all expenditure and falls hardest on those with lowest incomes.

Those who are in work and have rising incomes owe a debt to those out of work. The progressive reductions of trading barriers, both within the European Union and in the successive world trade agreements, have greatly increased international competition and, for those who can afford it, this has brought a far wider range of goods at lower prices. The rise in world trade has also been the main motor of growth for several decades.

The competition which has given us these benefits has also forced weaker companies out of business and has closed down industries which rely on cheap labour and forced us up-market. This is the main economic reason for the lack of unskilled jobs and the decline in heavy work for men. So there is a strong moral case for those who have benefited from this competition to help those who have suffered from it, and in particular for policies which will help to create employment, even if, for a time, these need higher taxes to help to reduce interest rates and promote investment.

Greed has also corrupted the ideals of professional management. The 'fat cats' in business are a terrible example to those who have to work for them. Management of companies is as much about leadership as about technical expertise. If people are motivated, they will work well, and if not, they will work badly. The relationship between owners, managers and workers should be a seamless web. If owners are only interested in managers who can produce short-term profits, then they can hardly be surprised if the managers take what money they can lay hands on themselves while the going is good and before the dividends run dry.

And if the owners allow managers the right to generous share options, so that they too are rewarded by short-term profits, then how can the average worker respect their leadership? What is the worker to think of the top management who increase the profits by wholesale redundancies, putting pressure on those left behind to work harder to make up the gaps and putting at risk the long-term future of the company which pays their wages?

A business is a team and in any team, as we have said above, motivation is everything and the tone has to be set at the top. I have probably visited more companies and walked round more shop floors than most people, and I have consistently found that the tone of the place always reflects the tone of the management and the economic performance seems also to depend on a collective sense of identity. The old kind of industry, in which workers were no more than cogs in the machine, has disappeared. Workers now are more educated, what we make is more complex and therefore success depends far more on the individual than it used to do on the automaton on the production line. Loyalty has to be earned and greed at the top is death to the enterprise.

The love of money

Greed tells us that money matters more than friends, more than family, more than reputation and that it can bring satisfaction and happiness which they cannot bring. It is one large lie. I once sat at a lunch near to Paul Getty, said to be the richest man in the world. He also looked the most miserable man I have ever seen in my life; it was written in every line in his deeply lined face. Not all rich people are as miserable as that, but riches can cut off those who have them from the warmth and humanity of life, from the breadth of friendship between those who are on equal terms. Money is at the heart of most family quarrels. The book of Ecclesiastes gives the views of a man who had everything, possibly Solomon, about the futility of wealth.

There was a discussion on TV about whether mothers with small children should go out to work. One woman said that she needed the money for her children. She said angrily that if she did not go out to work she would not have nearly so much to give them, so it was all for their benefit. It did not seem to have occurred to her that her little children might sooner have her than her presents.

There are all kinds of good reasons for mothers going out to work. Women who have skills, degrees and professions want to use them. But there is a time when little children want a mother, especially when their small lives feel blighted by some disaster and the need for a mother's comfort will not wait for 'quality time' a few hours later. Previous generations managed on lower incomes and more time with small children and so can we.

Men are as much to blame for putting money before family. A pastor I know has a church full of young professional families, where the husbands are never at home. It seems to be accepted that a high-flying professional husband must stay at work until nine at night, must be prepared to ring his wife to tell her to pack a suitcase, send it to his office in a taxi and expect him back on Friday. On Sunday afternoon the car comes to take him to the airport for another four or five days in Milan or wherever. And when these husbands do have time off, they are so out of touch with their families that they take their leisure activities by themselves. My pastor friend does not see how the marriage can hold together and worries at the problems with the children when they become teenagers. Above all, he thinks it quite unnecessary and I am sure that he is right.

Whatever the politicians may say, our insistence on tax-cutting above everything else puts the welfare state in danger. It is true that because medicine can do more for us than it used to, there are steadily increasing demands on the health service. Add an ageing population and it is no wonder that demands on the health service have gone up. So the health service is under continuous pressure to make offsetting cuts. But are we to say that people who can be cured will not be cured because we can no longer find the generosity in society to fund them?

The old-age pension will also be under pressure because the number of abortions have cut the birth-rate and there will soon be more pensioners and fewer earning the money needed to keep them. Already the pension is only just keeping up with the cost of living but not with the increase in earnings, so the gap is widening between those who are earning and paying low taxes and pensioners who, throughout their lives, paid far higher taxes and set the foundations for the wealth most people are enjoying today.

If government cannot change the balance between taxes and interest rates to encourage investment and improve the economy, two million unemployed will become two and a half or three million, and there will be less money to pay them for doing nothing than there is today. If marriages go on breaking up at the current rate, there will be more single parents and more claims on social security for the family. And if the divide between rich and poor goes on growing at the current rate, there will be greater problems of law and order and a much higher cost in police and prisons – though even that will not solve the problem. As a policeman in Bolton said, 'What is the good of one more of us if a hundred parents have given up?'

This takes no account of the cuts which have already been made, of the homeless stuck in bed-sits because local authorities were not allowed to use the proceeds of the sale of council houses to build more for those in need. There are those who may still have homes, but live in poverty with small children because their husbands cannot be made to pay the alimony. A woman opened a door in Peterborough with a paint-brush in her hand. She told us she had saved all year for the paint for the front room.

Then there are those who have been turned out of the mental hospitals and returned 'to the community'. We asked the staff in the crypt of St George's, Leeds, what they thought of 'care in the community'. They looked at us and said, 'What community?' The community does not want them and a large proportion of them drift at one time or another through the church doors, like St George's. We have three who come fairly regularly to our church and others who turn up from time to time. Sometimes, when the doors are open in the summer, we just hear the long wails of someone outside letting us know he is there. I asked one of the less frequent visitors how he was. He said, 'Not so good. I find it hard to get lodgings.' I asked why and he said, 'Because I'm violent. I can't help it, but they don't like it.'

Saddest of all is that there is a generation who say that their only hope is that they win the lottery. The propaganda for the lottery does not tell them that they are more likely to die tomorrow than they are to win the jackpot. The lottery is a method of funding public causes so that their cost can be kept off the national budget. When we look at the queue to buy tickets, they are those who can least afford it. But, as they say, in a materialistic world, where only money matters, it *is* their only hope.

We have only to look at America to see where we are heading. There the divide between the haves and the have-nots is already complete in every US city. There is a sharp two-class health service. Those with credit cards can get immediate treatment, those without have to wait and the public hospitals are awful. Violence is endemic in American cities and capital punishment seems to make no difference. The rich housing estates are increasingly circled by high fences and access is securely guarded.

Yet the right in American politics won the Congressional election in 1994 on the policy of budget cuts and in the 1996 election President Clinton followed them with a pledge to get welfare off the federal budget.

It does not have to go as far as that in Britain. But if our own nation loses its moral guidelines, we are wide open to the vested interests which put up a smoke-screen of argument whenever anyone proposes an answer to the problems which might be effective. So in looking at the arguments against change we must blow away these smoke-screens and insist on looking at all possible options. Above all, we need to recover the moral imperatives which have guided us for so long and taken us so far.

Chapter Six

How to restore full employment

One and a half million new jobs

The argument of the previous chapter would seem to justify the view widely held today that the full employment we enjoyed for twenty years after the war is no longer practicable. But it is a great mistake in life to start off with the problems, because the temptation is to turn problems into excuses for doing nothing. And, even if we do stir ourselves, we let the problems set the agenda. Instead we should start off by deciding where we would like to be if there were no difficulties so that the desirable objectives set the agenda, as they must. Only when we decide where we want to go do we look at what stands in the way.

At the time of writing we have over two million unemployed plus those not on the unemployment register who would like to work if they could. So the very first object of the exercise should be to create at least a million and a half worthwhile jobs. In 1955, when the postwar problems had worked themselves out and the economy was running normally, we had only a quarter of a million unemployed and those were mainly people who were changing jobs. So no more than half a million should be a sustainable objective.

Government would no longer need to pay a million and a half people to do nothing and would, instead, receive: the tax revenue from PAYE; as people spent more, from VAT; as profits rose, from company tax. The benefit to the Exchequer would be an estimated £26 billion. It would give government its only foreseeable opportunity both to cut taxes and also to spend more on education, health, housing and pensions. It would restore hope to areas where there is high unemployment and security to those who are now so worried that the job they have at the moment could soon disappear.

Recovering our trade surplus in manufactures

The first firm step towards full employment must be the recovery of our trade surplus in manufactures. We were the first great manufacturing country and we had an excess of exports over imports in manufactured goods until the early 1980s, when, as mentioned above, we lost it.

That first step would not now be enough on its own to recover all the employment which we lost in manufacturing, because industry is now capital-intensive and high-tech and uses machines more than muscle. But a surplus in manufacturing would allow us to pay for the extra imports needed if we expanded the big labour-intensive domestic industries such as construction and healthcare. And, since manufacturing exports give us twice as much currency revenue as exports of services, we have to expand there if we are to create employment anywhere else.

Two Oxford dons, Christine Greenhalgh and Mary Gregory, did an excellent paper for the 1994 TUC conference on 'Why manufacturing still matters' (published in 1996 by Routledge under the title 'Working for Full Employment'). They point out that four million manufacturing jobs have been lost since the 1960s, and that this deindustrialisation began earlier in Britain and has been more severe than in other manufacturing countries. 'The fall of 20 per cent in British manufacturing employment in under three years in the early 1980s has no parallel among the major economies.' So 'the development of policies to promote UK industry is a necessary part of a strategy for employment.' They say that we have lost our share of the market, while our main competitors have held or gained share. The lesson I draw is that we should try to regain some of the share which we have lost.

Gregory and Greenhalgh argue that manufacturing also matters because it is the main source of the increases in productivity which pay for necessary but expensive services and industries such as construction, where productivity rises more slowly. And, they point out, though fewer people are employed directly in manufacturing, it also pays the wages of all the industries which serve it, both service industries and subcontractors. When the major factory closes down in a middle-sized town it affects every business in the town. So a recovery in manufacturing spreads employment far and wide.

Some people argue that Britain should become a service economy. But our share of international trade in services has declined faster than our share of manufacturing, so it is no substitute. Though only 20 per cent of our employment is in manufacturing, it accounts for 60 per cent of our exports. It is far easier to import and export goods than services. Only 20 per cent of service output can be exported, and the same goes for imports. You don't see foreign construction companies' signs on our building sites. It's still Wimpey, Laing and Costain. Nor do you see Commerzbank on the high street. But Sony is everywhere. Growth since the war has been fuelled by the lowering of barriers to international trade and we are all far better off, including the poor countries with which we trade.

Investment needs stable currency and low interest rates

So why did we lose ground in manufacturing and how can we win it back again? I spent long years of my life in the public service, under both Labour and Conservative governments. Greenhalgh and Gregory have, in my view, got it right. They point the finger at 'fluctuating exchange rates which are damaging to business-making' and say that 'British industry has been handicapped by higher interest rates and, more generally, by a higher cost of capital than major competitors.'

We hear a lot about the need to keep wage rates competitive. But our wage rates are already lower than those of our main competitors. Low wages are no substitute for investment. As industry becomes more capital-intensive, it is the cost of capital which is critical rather than the cost of labour. Of course no businessman wants to pay more than he need for anything, including labour. But even if a business were paying coolie wages, it still could not compete unless it had the money to invest in new products. And new technology needs money not only for plant, but also for both research and development, in which our major competitors also invest much more heavily than we do.

We do not have to look far for the reason for this higher rate of investment. The cost of corporate bonds is 40 per cent higher for British companies than it is for their main continental competitors. So, for the same cash cost, Britain's main competitors can put down 40 per cent more investment in new products than a British company and they can keep or improve their share of the market despite their higher cost of wages. That is the heart of the matter.

The reason for the premium is simple. Our main competitors have been part of the stable European Monetary System (EMS) since 1979 and do not have to allow, as we do, for the risk of a fluctuating exchange rate when they decide to invest. They have another advantage: that unstable exchange rates are a source of inflation, another investment risk, and investors in British companies have to allow for this risk too.

The removal of this bias against investment in British industry would lower the cost of finance and should enable British companies to invest 40 per cent more for the same interest cost. The only action we can take to persuade currency and money markets that these risks have been removed permanently is to join our continental partners in their proposal for a permanent fixing of their currencies.

European Monetary Union is the key

This solution to this enormous bias against investment in Britain is on offer: it is European Monetary Union, agreed in the Maastricht Treaty and ratified by national parliaments (with an opt-out for Britain) in the belief that a single European market needs a single European currency. That would not only remove the exchange risk with the market on which we depend for 60 per cent of our exports. It would also, on the terms of Monetary Union, curb the unprecedented inflation from which we have been suffering since the 1960s. If we take the opt-out, we not only lose all that; we are faced across the channel with a currency which is then far stronger, more widely held and much more attractive to capital, and while they will have even lower interest rates, ours will have to be much higher than they are now to prevent a flight of capital from Britain.

It is argued that the loss of a national currency takes away our sovereignty. In all my thirty years in public life, from 1964 to 1994, I have never seen the free exercise of British sovereignty. The power over our post-war currency was held first by the Americans, when we were tied to the dollar; then by the currency speculators; or, if we wanted to be rescued from them, by the International Monetary Fund (IMF). Today it is held by the Bundesbank, who have been persuaded by the German government to give it up. That offer will not be repeated, which is why all the other countries in Europe are desperate to join, even if it means a tighter budget. If it were really an economic benefit to us to have a floating currency, we should have done better than all our continental competitors. As it is, those with the fixed currencies have done far better and we have done far worse.

The only sovereignty at issue is the sovereign power of a British government to devalue the pound. That is the power which enables governments in office to bribe the electorate with its own money. So, small wonder that there is a fuss about the prospect of their losing it! They cannot, of course, use that as an argument. They have to use, instead, a free-standing argument which has no economic logic attached, so they wrap themselves round with the Union Jack and talk the language of nationalism.

What we need to note is that export industry and the trades unions – those who are most involved and have most directly at stake – are in favour of our being in the European Monetary Union.

The moral and economic case for ending inflation

The conditions set for the European Monetary System are deliberately tough on inflation. The German government could not persuade the German people to part with the D-Mark unless it had the same tough rules against governments which raise money by borrowing instead of taxation. And the Germans are right. Inflation is not just an economic issue, it is a moral issue too; for inflation falls hardest on those who are not able to defend themselves, the people at the bottom, the unemployed, the poor and those who do not have the power to make sure that their earnings keep up with inflation.

Inflation is the cruellest tax, for it falls on everyone alike and there are no exemptions for old age or poverty. It is divisive, for it sets class against class, trades union against trades union, general worker against skilled. But, above all, it takes away from the elected government the power to control the economy, since a slippery sliding pound puts everything up for grabs. It takes £11 today to buy what £1 could have bought in 1961. It is time that chronic inflation came to an end.

But inflation is a drug and the process of detoxification, which the Maastricht Treaty has set in motion, is hard. People are used to governments which print money to get out of short-term problems. It is to the credit of courageous politicians that they are prepared to see the process through.

Eating the seed-corn

The problem of ownership without responsibility, which we discussed in the last chapter, makes it especially difficult for British export industry to match the investment of our major international competitors. In continental Europe, at least a quarter of the shares in the big export companies are in the hands of owners with a long-term interest in the future of the company and, when they are persuaded that a long-term investment is worth making, they will give it their backing until it pays off, even if interest charges on the new venture reduce the profits meantime. So the management may have a tough time before the owners agree, but then they can get on with the job.

In Britain and the United States, by contrast, shares in public companies are very widely held and there is, as we have seen, great pressure from shareholders for short-term profits. As a result company boards are limited to investments which will produce a big immediate return, regardless of the loss of their share of the market. This has been spelt out most dramatically by Will Hutton, now editor of the *Observer*, in his bestseller, *The State We're In*. He has been harsh in his criticisms of the City and it has responded with outrage.

Without something like the continental structure, where large shareholders organise themselves to look after their long-term interests, the City is wide open to the short-term pressures of our materialistic society, which wants the highest possible return on its money today. I had a long talk to the general manager of one of the major pension companies and complained about the pressure which financial institutions like his put on industrial companies for short-term profits. He pointed out that they too were under pressure from insurance brokers. To sell their pension policies, they had to show that the market value of the shares they held was rising faster than that of other pension funds.

I talked to an old friend who is a pension broker and put the same point to him. He said that his clients wanted to see that their money was in funds which performed well and that the only visible indication of performance was share price. If he put their money into funds which did not have such a good performance, he was, under the latest laws, liable to be sued for negligence. He said that when the Morgan Grenfell fund had lost its assets after an apparently record performance, he did a check and found that ten of his clients were in the fund, but not on his advice. All of them had insisted that he invest their money in Morgan Grenfell because they had read about its sparkling performance.

Until the mid-1960s, it was rare for directors to take much notice of the share price. They took the view that it went up and down with the mood of the market. The level of the share price was not part of their legal responsibility as directors. Their duty to the shareholders who elected them was to use their assets to get the optimum economic performance and they let the market look after the share price.

The coming of hostile takeover bids changed this view. If bidders thought that the shares were a bargain and that they could improve their value by better use of the assets, then the directors would speedily find themselves without a job. There was no point in attending to the long-term position, because unless they survived the bid, they would not be there in the long term. Hostile takeover bids are finance driven and it does not seem to matter that the bidders know nothing about the business they are taking over – at least not until their conglomerate starts to unravel.

To keep themselves clear of predators it was necessary for companies to make sure that their share price was as high as it could be. But heavy investment in new products which were needed to keep their place in the market would bring heavy interest charges for several years before they paid off. That depressed profits and made the company vulnerable to a hostile bid. Heavy investment in a big new smelter was the undoing of the British Aluminium Company, which was taken over in the biggest hostile bid to date in 1959.

Yet the biggest shareholders, the pension funds, are holding their investments against long-term liabilities. So there is no reason other than pressure from brokers and their clients for them to take a short-term view; no reason to sell out to a bidder for short-term profits; no reason to finance bidders who know nothing about the business they are buying. And, since continental European countries and Japan do not suffer from these short-term pressures, there must be a better way of financing the long-term investment in our vital export industries.

In the report to the 1996 congress on 'stakeholding', the TUC have made some compelling arguments for change. They point out that investment in manufacturing remains 22 per cent below the pre-recession level and that, even now, five years into the recovery, investment has not returned to its level at the low point of the recession. So, clearly something has to be done to change this trend.

They believe that managements themselves are now far too heavily geared to the market performance of their shares, against the long-term interest of the company and those who work in it. They say that 90 per cent of companies operate share option schemes which give executives large returns from the growth of the share price. This has as much to do with the share of profits paid out in dividends (roughly doubled in the 1980s) as with the performance of the company. The higher dividends also leave less to be put back in new investment in the business. They contrast this with German and Japanese firms where the ratio paid out in dividend is only half that of the UK.

The TUC say that in the latest takeover boom, UK firms spent £32 billion on takeovers within the UK in 1995 – £5 billion more than in the last peak in 1989 – that research by independent academics and government shows that takeovers have little or no beneficial economic effect and that the fear of takeover creates pressure on managers to keep their share price high and diverts their attention from the real business of competitiveness.

They clearly believe that this has something to do with the pattern of ownership, where British industry has two thousand firms quoted on the stock exchange compared with fewer than seven hundred in Germany and five hundred in France. And the 60 per cent of UK shares owned by institutional investors are spread thinly across a large number of firms, whereas in Germany and France there is usually a principal shareholder or group of shareholders who control ownership and 80 per cent of companies have at least one shareholder owning 25 per cent of the equity. So German and French shareholders are nearer to their companies, more involved in the decisions they make and in a better position to protect them from hostile bids. It is their higher rate of investment which has kept them competitive until now despite their higher wage costs.

The TUC propose legal changes which would be large enough to arouse fierce opposition in the City, but would not be enough to make boards more secure in putting down long-term investment.

I believe that we have to base a new system on the principle that power carries responsibility and that voting rights should not be held except by those who are prepared, in one way or another, to commit themselves to the good of the corporate whole, including its employees. The first principle of leadership is that allegiance has to be earned by the commitment of leaders to those for whom they are responsible. It will not be earned by 'fat cats'.

The old entrepreneurs who built our companies up were leaders who knew that they had to command that allegiance, and those who worked for them knew who was ultimately responsible. While anonymous shareholders were prepared to let professional management (people like the late Lord Heywood of Unilever) take the place of the founders, there was no problem. But when the invisible owners clearly did not care a fig about the long-term future of the company; when, regardless of the future of the company, they systematically removed boards who did not give first priority to higher dividends; those vulnerable directors forfeited their respect as leaders. The TUC are right to call attention to the damage to employees and to the country; but effective change needs the backing of a much wider constituency and that needs agreement on the principle that power and responsibility must go together.

The need for an economic forum

During the years when I was in public service, these issues would have been discussed on the National Economic Development Council between a government team of the six economic ministers headed by the chancellor or prime minister, six from the Confederation of British Industry (CBI), six from the TUC, three independent members and the director general of NEDC, a post I held for five years of my seven years as a member.

The NEDC did not depend on the government for its input but on the committees for each major industry, which had parallel constitutions and were chaired by a respected industrialist or trades unionist. This prevented it from being just a clash of interests at the highest level. It was not an executive body. It could not prevent the government from carrying out its electoral mandate. But it did provide a highly informed and solidly experienced forum of able debaters – Alf Robens, Frank Kearton, John Davies, Vic Feather, Les Cannon, Jack Jones, Tony Crosland, Roy Jenkins, Edward Heath – each capable of pinning down their opponents in argument and, in the process, coming out with agreements which all could live with and support.

These were not easy debates, because they were not just a meeting of experts. We had the views of the experts and our object was to hammer out an agreement which we could defend to our very different constituencies. Its great merit is that we could all see what was politically possible and what was not and what would have to be conceded by each section to gain agreement. Yet, looking back, the agreements we forged were a great deal more successful in achieving our objectives than anything that has happened since.

During my seven years on the council we had the EEC tariffs against us and yet, in what we all recognised as a collective effort, we managed to go from a huge payments deficit in 1964 to a respectable trade and payments surplus in 1970. The rate of inflation, interest rates and unemployment were all low. And the industry committees spread the feeling that we all had a stake in a united national effort.

The issues before the council set the agenda for the wider national debate and, because the NEDC was not putting a spin on stories, it became a reliable checkpoint for journalists, so the issues were debated on their merits and not as a part of the party political or union/management argument.

Today it is almost impossible to find a public argument on the real issues which face the country. The TV soundbites on St Stephen's Green are not arguments; they are unsubstantiated assertions from prejudiced backbenchers of opposing views. Even BBC's *Newsnight*, with its late-night forty-five minutes, is not much better. Politicians have mastered the art. They answer a question which has not been asked and they know that if they don't stop talking, the interviewer will run out of time before getting them into difficulties. It is marginally better than the two-party House of Commons, but not in getting an informed public debate on critical issues and certainly not in changing opinion among those who create our wealth.

It must now be clear to all who look at the figures that government has policies to get people back to work; or will have to raise taxes to support them; or, worst of all, will have to do what President Clinton has now proposed: take a substantial number of people off welfare. Yet we are now in an extraordinary situation where the opposition refuses to challenge government in case it is asked what it would do when in power. So there is no forum in which there can be an informed debate on the economic future of our country, and the opposition vacuum is being filled by the dogmas of the English nationalist wing of the Conservative Party.

The Thatcherite theory was that the market looked after all economic problems. That theory has now had a fair trial over eighteen years. But even with the huge infusion of revenue and hard currency from North Sea oil, it has clearly failed in every area: employment, industrial investment, trade surplus and inflation.

In our industrial economy, where jobs depend on our economic success, the market needs a forum in which government and industry can debate together. Those who have the political power and those who have the economic power need to talk for their mutual benefit, and not least for the instruction of ministers whose experience in their office is unlikely to be more than two years. Politicians are good at setting out their aims. But business deals with hard realities and wants to know not only what their governments' economic aims are, but how exactly they propose to achieve them.

Ad hoc consultation with industry is not at all the same thing as a round-table debate, one which aims to achieve the industrial confidence needed for higher investment and more jobs. The European Union is a highly competitive market, and if we do not make the investment needed to keep our share then we will continue to lose out to those who do. For over twenty years we have tried to have it both ways: to be in but not committed; to open our markets, but not make the investment for the markets open to us; to lower tariff barriers, but to keep unique currency barriers which weaken our own business. The forum in which all these urgent points need to be debated has been silenced. It needs to come to life again.

Europe as the motor of growth

Our major European partners also have a large problem of unemployment. The long recession of the early 1990s was caused by the union of West Germany with the shattered economy of East Germany. The Germans, in their systematic way, set out to rebuild the new Eastern provinces and used the strength of the D-Mark to borrow most of the huge sums needed. This put up interest rates across Europe and brought the expansion of the late 1980s to an abrupt end. The inclusion of the East German unemployed gives the Germans a special problem of high unemployment. Spain is another country with a similar problem.

Quite apart from the considerable benefit to Britain, it is calculated by Christopher Johnson, former economic adviser to Lloyds Bank, that monetary union would raise the whole of Europe's annual growth rate to a steady 2.75 to 3 per cent. Lower cross-border costs would increase trade and it would lower real (post-inflation) interest rates from 4 to 3 per cent. This would make capital cheaper and create more investment and more jobs. Beyond that, we need a European Union commitment to full employment and an institution at European level with power to achieve it.

The European Union has had a bad press in Britain over the years and the anti-European drumbeat from our foreign-owned national press has been going on for so long that readers may be left with the feeling that no good can come out of Europe. But the long British tradition has been to complain about Europe and then find that we have to go along with it. It is, in my fifteen years' experience in Strasbourg and Brussels, far better to get in there and where there is a common interest, such as high unemployment, make sure that we have united European policies which can put it right.

It is more difficult to get agreement at European level, but when you do get it, it is ten times as effective and it sticks. The single European market was a European Parliament initiative which brought to an end the stagnation of the early 1980s and gave us a million new jobs in Britain alone.

What we need now is another such initiative. More than Europe depends on it. Europe has to take over as the motor economy of world trade, since the US is too deeply in deficit and Japan too small. The EU is two-thirds as big now as the US, and what the US did in the past we should certainly be able to do now.

My last effort at the European Parliament, in 1993/4, was to try to get agreement on an aid package which would start up the economies of Russia and the Ukraine. They had collapsed because half of their industry was producing armaments and the other half could no longer support it. They cannot get back on to their feet again without outside help and the loans on offer from the International Monetary Fund will not do anything to get the huge number of displaced workers from the defence industries into productive work.

The amount on offer from the IMF was a loan of $1.5 billion. Even this was conditional on their curbing inflation by themselves, which they could not do. The World Bank estimate for the amount they needed for temporary help for the unemployed was $15 billion. For comparison, American help for Western Europe after World War II was $75 billion and the annual amount we were still spending in NATO on cold war weaponry and research was $150 billion.

So the European Parliament called for a Marshall Aid package, to be funded by the running down of the manufacture of NATO's very expensive cold war weapon production and to be paid to former defence companies to make the machinery which the Russians and Ukranians would need to equip themselves to improve their agriculture, forestry and oil and coal production and transport, so that they could become a major trading partner of the West.

I paid two visits to Moscow and, at a remarkable all-day meeting, the Russian defence industry – though they would have liked to do it all themselves – admitted that they needed help. We had a two-day hearing in Brussels to test the feasibility of the project. Western defence industry thought it was both feasible and desirable. My opposite numbers in the US Congress liked it. The chairman of the Senate Armed Services Committee, Sam Nunn, pointed out that he and Senator Lugar had done something similar on a smaller scale; but the parliamentary term was nearly over, so we ran out of time and the new Congress was not so helpful.

Meantime the governments of the West have sat on their hands at enormous risk to the stability not only of Eastern Europe, but of Central Europe too. The old nomenklatura have taken over the assets of Russian industry and are keeping the hard currency from their exports. The mafia have sprung up to take their rake-off from these new riches. The Russian Parliament was shelled and a more compliant parliament set up instead. But the government can no longer raise taxes and the army is not being paid. No one can afford to recondition the score of Chernobyl-type power stations which are still running nor deal with any of the other dangerous nuclear waste. Lech Walesa, when President of Poland, had told us in his usual blunt manner, 'If they collapse in the East and come over the Polish frontier, I can do nothing. I'll pass them straight on to you.' He exaggerated, but only up to a point. Instability in Eastern Europe destabilises Central Europe.

I was told by a senior British politician that Eastern Europe was a 'black hole'. But the World Bank has vast experience in seeing that aid goes to the proper destination in a lot of corrupt economies round the world. And even if it were an economic risk, the political risk of nuclear weapons falling into the hands of local warlords or of a major collapse in Russia is even greater. We should know from the consequences of the Versailles Treaty that it does not pay to put to shame a great country which has lost a war, and the example of Germany today shows the great benefit of treating a vanquished nation well.

A growth of trade with Eastern Europe would do far more for our economies than the manufacture of cold war weaponry – which is certainly of little use in the kind of conflicts which have succeeded the cold war. Weapons, unlike products bought for their intrinsic value, are not a multiplier of trade. They contribute nothing to our daily needs and end up either stored or destroyed.

Eastern trade may take time to develop, but it would give the biggest surge forward in trade that we can hope for, and as we geared up for this surge it would affect our economy fairly quickly, giving new life and hope to towns vulnerable to the cutbacks in defence. So it should have the full and positive attention of a British government, which should take it up both in NATO and in the European Union. It is not yet too late.

Training

We would not know, until the economy expanded, whether we had enough skilled workers, but those with their ears to the Treasury door hear the view that we would only be able to get unemployment down by two hundred thousand before the economy began to overheat because of lack of skilled workers. The old industry councils have gone and Training and Enterprise Councils (TECs) have taken their place. But the TECs do not seem to be in a position to run ahead of likely current demand, and in any case industrialists find that it is not easy to persuade people to take training when there do not seem to be any jobs at the end of the training period.

If there were an economic forum, including the trades unions, this is one of the first problems it should tackle. As a country we have been backward in our training of skilled workers, and it would be surprising if with the decline of manufacturing there had not also been a decline in the number of skilled workers. We cannot have expansion of the economy unless we have the skills, so industrial training should be a matter of urgency for government.

The need for flexibility in taxation

If the European Monetary Union goes ahead and Britain commits itself to be in the first wave, it will help to reduce the damaging differential between the cost of investment in Britain and Continental Europe. But if there is any hiccup then, to encourage investment, government should raise taxes and lower interest rates.

There is nothing very complex about the economics of this change. All else being equal, the more government borrows, the higher the interest rates and the lower the rate of new industrial investment. If government pays its way by raising taxation then it does not have to borrow so much, interest rates go down and investment goes up.

So if those who are in jobs and earning are successful in putting pressure on political parties to lower their taxes, this has a damaging effect on the rate of investment and the level of employment. No party should give in to this pressure and any new government should keep this option open. And those who want to see the shame of unemployment brought to an end should point out that the only way in which the burden of public expenditure can be lifted and taxes lowered in the long term is to get people back to work. To take away government's flexibility in taxation is the road to ruin.

Chapter Seven

WHO WANTS FULL EMPLOYMENT
– AND WHO DOESN'T

Is there really a problem?

The general assumption of both major political parties is that the British economy is heading roughly in the right direction and that marginal adjustment will see us through. That is dangerous nonsense.

It is nonsense first of all because the claims on government are not stable. They are going to increase. Because of the high abortion rate our birth-rate has dropped and because of better health, people are living longer. In 1961 the population over 65 was only 12 per cent, in 1994 it was 18 per cent and in 2031 it is reckoned to be 23 per cent of the total. So the cost of pensions relative to earned income is going up and up. Second, the amount spent on our whole social security budget is also going up sharply, from 27 per cent of the budget in 1981 to 34 per cent in 1994. Third, health service costs have gone up from 11 per cent of the budget to 14 per cent. Fourth, the polls tell us that nearly three-quarters of the voters now want more money to be spent not only on pensions, but also on education and police. They are right. We certainly need to spend more, not less, to achieve the standards of education and training which are vital if we are to keep our edge in high-tech competition. And with unemployment between 30 per cent and 50 per cent in our great city estates, the cost of law and order is also rising fast.

Governments may talk about slashing this cost or that, but they never do it because the money they are spending is meeting a real need. This is especially apparent when politicians are asked where the money is going to be found for the tax cuts which they promise in the near future and cannot tell us. So all the signs are that, without a fundamental change of policies, government expenditure will grow. Either we need higher taxes or we need a fundamental change of economic policy. That change can only come from a new economic package which gives us an export surplus strong enough to expand the economy, reduce unemployment and give us again the buoyant revenue to meet all these needs. But a change of policy will need higher tax in the short run.

That new policy will not come with a little trimming here and a little there, followed by a long, long wait for the economy to turn round. The package needs to be strong enough to switch our resources out of the utterly unproductive business of paying two million people for doing nothing, and into an investment in British industry and commerce sufficient to restore the share of world trade back to the level of the late seventies, when we were beginning to take the share of the European market proper to our size and industrial experience.

The major parties play on the popular assumption that, since we had a good time in the 1980s, it should not be so hard to get back to those conditions now. But there is no point in looking back to the eighties as a golden age when we had all the answers. The high spending and feel-good factor of the eighties were the result of a one-off trade surplus in oil and a non-recurring £43 billion of extra hard currency income which enabled us to pay for our high personal consumption and to ride out the severe damage of the over-valued pound to our export business and the resultant three million unemployed. In the mid-eighties we lived on the left-over currency surplus and in the late eighties we went deep into debt.

Today these resources have gone and we continue to be crippled by the annual £26 billion cost to the Exchequer of continuing high unemployment, not counting the forfeit of about 5 per cent to the national product if the majority of the unemployed were back at work. So we cannot meet the future with the policies of the eighties.

Without strong new policies the British economy will get worse, not better. We are now down a dead end and we have to find a way out. We should also look to see how other countries are trying to solve the same problems today and look back on our solutions in the sixties and seventies, before the high pound knocked our industry endways and the oil surplus enabled us to ignore our difficulties.

The urgent need for a new economic package

What we have to have from an incoming government after the next election is a concerted programme powerful enough to achieve the major switch of resources to bring a million and a half people back to work. As we look again at our own past achievements and outwards at what other countries are doing now, the package begins to spell itself out.

There are those who will label any economic package as 'socialist planning'. Despite everything, their faith still rests on an unfettered market economy and they believe that it will always do damage to interfere with the market, whether by fixing currencies or by preferring one section of the economy over another. If the country runs a deficit, it simply borrows to finance it. It was that philosophy which, under President Reagan, turned the United States from the world's largest creditor nation into the world's largest debtor. But no other country, except Britain, has been foolish enough or strong enough to follow that example.

Britain before the oil boom and most of our competitor countries today have made the achievement of a foreign trading surplus their first priority. A country in debt is at the mercy of exchange markets, has to pay an interest rate premium for foreign loans and accept whatever conditions are imposed in return for support of its currency. If the pressure is too great and the currency drops sharply, import costs rise and start a wage–price spiral. The strength of the D-Mark rests on the trading surplus of Germany. So it follows that countries have to give priority to the sector which earns their foreign currency.

Nearly two-thirds of Britain's exports are from manufactures and, until the eighties, Britain had a consistent surplus in trade in manufacturing. In the early eighties, our share of world trade dropped by over 20 per cent, our surplus disappeared and the rate of new investment in plant and machinery did not recover its 1979 level until the height of the Lawson boom in 1988. By 1989 Britain's surplus on visible trade had not only disappeared, the deficit had plunged to an incredible £23 billion. In market after market we did not have the plant to match the next generation of new products and in 1992 our rate of new investment was back below the 1979 level.

Investment in manufacturing industry matters. An old Dutch merchant once told me, 'You British are the most inventive people in the world and we love your prototypes; but you do not put your money behind your own inventions. Someone else invests in the idea and we have to deal with them and not with you.' I do not see how we can fight our way back without a substantial increase in the capacity of our manufacturing industry. As argued above, its exports are twice as large as 'invisible' exports and far more tradeable.

The monetarists complain that to look after British export industry demands an artificial subsidy. But industry does not need subsidy; all it needs are competitive conditions. British industrial investment has been low because Britain is outside the European Monetary System, and British interest rates have had to carry a risk premium both on the rate of inflation and on the value of the currency. The result of this double risk is, as we saw in the last chapter, to add 40 per cent to the cost of raising industrial capital.

Since competitive interest rates need either fixed exchange rates or higher taxes to bring down government's borrowing, both of which are against monetarist theory, they concentrate on the need for a competitive cost of labour. It seems to escape their notice that British wage rates are already well below the level of all those countries which have done far better in world trade than Britain. So they turn their fire on the continental practice of adding social costs of employment as a 50 per cent surcharge on the wage rate. Recently this practice has done great damage and, for that reason, the current rate of unemployment on the continent is higher than ours. But putting the charge on employers instead of meeting it through general taxation is only one means of raising the money. There is no need for Britain to change our practice, even if we do sign the famous Social Chapter of Maastricht. So the argument remains that, for an advanced industrial country, low wages are no alternative to competitive equipment. All the most successful countries in international trade have a high-investment, high-wage economy.

As modern industry has become more capital-intensive, there has been a steady drop in the direct wage content and, in all industrial countries, there has also been a steady rise in output in manufacturing with a steady drop in numbers employed.

So our problem is not with the people, but with the lack of equipment. Just as you cannot expect soldiers to win their battles unless they have the tanks, planes and missiles to match the other side, so we cannot expect our industries to keep market share in the nineties with the equipment and products of the sixties and seventies. New products need high costs in development and in the equipment to make them. And if exporters cannot afford to match their competitors' investment and lose out on the next generation of products because they do not have the equipment, they will not be able to recover the markets they have lost. That is my consistent experience as an industrialist, as chairman of the British Overseas Trade Board and as an MEP for the very successful high-tech industry in my Cambridgeshire constituency.

So there is no valid objection that I can see to an economic package which aims to ensure that we have a competitive manufacturing industry, able to raise its capital on equal terms with its major international competitors.

Foreign investment in Britain

The monetarists argue that if it is so expensive to raise money in Britain, how is it that we attract more foreign investment than any other country in Europe? There are several reasons for high foreign investment in Britain. One is that English is the international language of commerce and it is easier for American companies to work in a country where their managers can understand the language without difficulty. The same may go for the Japanese, whose main second language is English. Also, the two British industries with incorrigibly bad management in the sixties and seventies were the car and newspaper industries and the Japanese and Americans have stepped into the gap. The vastly improved car industry is now wholly owned by Americans, Japanese and Germans; and the rebuilt newspaper industry is dominated by an American and a Canadian. Japanese investment in the car industry was also aimed to overcome the quotas which the EU had put on the import of cars from Japan.

But we should not be too dependent on foreign investment for our future. Other countries – the Germans, the French, the Japanese – would not take this kind of dominance in their industries lightly and it should not become a habit with us. The success of British industry is a vital national interest and foreign owners are a great deal more footloose than British owners. The foreign plant is the first to be closed in a downturn, the least likely to do its own research and the most likely to import expensive components; and subsidiaries of foreign multinationals can use transfer pricing to reduce the taxes paid in Britain. Though we have always welcomed inward investment, we should not be dependent on it. British industry should be able to depend on British savings.

Those who boast about the rate of foreign investment in Britain are often the very same people who would damage British industry and deter foreign investment by excluding Britain from European Monetary Union. If that goes ahead, as seems likely, and we are excluded, it is almost certain that foreign investment in Britain will drop sharply.

The only practical way of removing the risk of exchange rate changes and higher interest rates from investment in Britain is to have the same currency as our main European competitors. That is why neither Conservatives nor New Labour will rule out British participation in monetary union. Only in a monetary union will we be able to put down investment for new products at the same rate as our main competitors, balance our trade and expand our economy. The French, who well understand their own interests, are determined that monetary union shall succeed and because money markets believe this, the French rates of interest are nearly as low as the key German rates, to the great advantage of French industry.

Christopher Johnson, whom I mentioned in the last chapter, is quite sure that monetary union is in both French and German interests. He quotes a leading French authority on his government's foreign policy as saying that each government wants what it does not have, 'France wants a currency and Germany a foreign policy'. That is the bargain and it is likely to be kept. When this happens, Holland, Belgium and Luxembourg will certainly join and that will represent half of the enormous EU market. Spain and Italy are also making strenuous efforts to see that their economies are in the right shape to join.

Were we not to go in at the same time, sterling would be faced with a currency far more extensive and powerful than the D-Mark, and the premium which British industry would have to pay for capital would be far more than the present 40 per cent. The advocates of a sovereign pound never tell us what rate of interest might be required to persuade the British and other holders to keep their money in pounds sterling, when they could invest in Euros, which would be far more tradeable than the old D-Mark and proofed against devaluation by the combined reserves of Europe.

We are bound to conclude that the main case against monetary union is not economic; it is nationalistic. The pound sterling, one of the most devalued currencies in the industrial world, has been elevated to the status of the Crown or Parliament for party political reasons.

Inflation

Nor does the argument for doing nothing take account of Britain's abysmal record of inflation. For the last few years, inflation has been low and this argument assumes that it has at last been conquered. But, as we mentioned above, the Treasury is said to believe that, were we to get only an extra two hundred thousand people back to work, the economy would overheat and we would run into inflation again.

Our two-year membership of the European Monetary System was enough to break the inflationary spiral. Since then our inflation has been restrained, despite the devaluation of 1992, by the long depression of the 1990s and the structural changes made by industry, but probably even more by the continued high rate of unemployment and the fear of worse to come.

Were we to stay out of monetary union on the grounds that we had to retain the right to devalue the pound, that would send the worst possible signals to currency markets. Sterling would, once more, have the reputation of a chronically weak currency and would, sooner or later, put pressure on the pound; we would be back on the old wage–price spiral which did so much damage in the 1960s, 1970s and 1980s, with high interest rates and continued fiscal restraint.

Most of my time in public life has coincided with sterling crises, when the currency markets continually tripped up the efforts of British governments to run a stable economy. There was not much evidence of sovereignty! They all caused a sharp rise in interest rates, which could defend sterling only by attacking the real economy and depressing the rate of new investment. The effect of inflation on business is to reinforce the temptation to insist on high returns on their investment and short payback periods and to avoid the long-term commitments needed to make the economy grow. Once in these cycles, it is very hard to get out of them.

Capital markets tend to believe that the pound is an inherently inflationary currency which needs high interest rates and inflationary wage settlements to cover the risk to investors and employees. In the mid-eighties when the tailing off of the oil surplus had brought the pound down to a more competitive level, and by a unique coincidence the dollar in which so many of our imports are priced came down as well, I tried to argue that there was no longer any need for inflationary wage awards, but the inflationary reputation of the pound was so firmly ingrained that unions insisted on awards to cover future inflation and employers conceded.

I spoke in 1986 at the annual meeting of the Advisory, Conciliation and Arbitration Service (ACAS), where both sides of wage negotiations were represented, and made the case for non-inflationary settlements. I also talked to the management of Ford on one of their visits to the European Parliament. It was clear from both encounters that the reputation of the pound for chronic inflation was deeply ingrained – and the belief was

113

self-fulfilling. Inflation went on for the next four years until the pound was worth only half its value when the Conservatives came to power and was slowed only when Britain entered the European Monetary System in 1990.

To me the very clear lesson is that if we are to get a million people back to work – let alone the million and a half which would bring us back to the more civilised levels of full employment – we will not do it on a vulnerable national currency; we need a European currency backed by a European central bank.

Why the opposition?

If higher growth is better for business and better for jobs, we have to ask ourselves why there is such opposition. Is it rational and, if so, are the reasons self-interested or sound? Perhaps it would be better to look first for the points of support. The people who know most about it are the British exporters and these are mainly large companies. In the opinion polls, the large companies come out heavily in favour. In a recent poll by Anderson Consulting, they were 58 per cent in favour and only 12 per cent against.

The TUC are also in favour. The workers want to be paid in wages which will hold their value. And, as I know from the chronic inflation in my time in public service, the risk of inflation makes the job of the trades union leaders ten times more difficult. Their members are driven by the fear that they will lose their differentials, that they do not have the bargaining power to keep up. If negotiation is in a hard currency, it removes the risks and most of the problems of collective bargaining. And the TUC also know that pre-election boom and subsequent bust have done no good for the British economy.

The Liberal Democrats are whole-heartedly in favour and, though they do not have many seats in parliament, they had fifteen million votes in the last election – more than a third of the Conservative total and nearly half of the Labour total. So we should not forget them. And, though the Labour Party are shy of commitment on a subject made so controversial by the Conservative backbenchers, it is my view that, for the same reasons as the TUC, they are in favour too. Finally there is a poll which gives half the

Cabinet as being in favour; which, considering the balance on their backbenches, is remarkable and one reason why the Conservatives adamantly refuse to rule out British membership.

There is, no doubt, some genuine anxiety that the 'rust belt' of Britain – the areas which have suffered from closures of old industries and have worse than average unemployment – might suffer if devaluation of the pound were removed as an instrument of government policy.

I was parliamentary rapporteur on this issue in the run-up to Maastricht, and we held a hearing with an excellent witness who had been a member of the Padoa–Schioppa Committee which had reported on the issue. Their view was that the key asset in the industrial regions of Europe was the tradition of the skilled worker, and that new industries which needed skill would far sooner invest in the old skilled areas than where there was no tradition of skill. This is what was happening in America, which has one currency but great diversity of skill between regions. But their single currency helped new investment for semi-skilled workers outside the old industrial areas, especially in the South. The Padoa–Schioppa Committee thought that a single currency would encourage investment in plants producing less sophisticated products in marginal areas in Europe.

The other answer to this anxiety is that the devaluation of the pound settles nothing. The response is a higher rate of inflation, with higher interest rates and lower investment. So poorer regions are no better off. That is the system we have had and it has not helped poorer regions.

There are those who worry about the limitations on national borrowing which are a precondition for membership. But what is happening here is that the member states are being made to do what they ought to do in any case, to bring their borrowing within non-inflationary limits. If we are to kill inflation and have a currency which keeps its value, we have got to stop borrowing beyond the increase justified by economic growth. That can hurt, but it is worth it for the reward of much lower interest rates and substantially higher growth which it brings. We have tried the current system and it does not work. We can look at those whose currencies are hard and see that they are far better off. The transfer from our failed system to their successful one is well worth the limitations on borrowing. Inflation as we have said is an indiscriminate tax, enabling government to raise revenue by stealth and falling hardest on those least able to bear it.

The real reason for the opposition, in my view, is that a large section of the Conservative Party believe that playing the nationalist card gives their best chance of regaining power. It used to be the Conservative and Unionist Party. It is increasingly the English Nationalist Party. To get the full flavour of this shift one has to move outside England and talk to the Welsh or the Scots and the Germans. They are in no doubt. Even those of us who are British-born, who have lived in England most of our lives though we are not ethnically English, and have never given the matter a thought; we are beginning to feel a discomfort we never felt before.

Conservative opposition to the monetary union can hardly be on the merits of the case. John Major got a mandate from parliament before he went to Maastricht; his policy was endorsed by parliament when he came back; he put it in the election manifesto and fought and won the election; and the policy was endorsed by the new parliament. Then a minority of the party started to oppose the treaty as it went through parliament for one long hot summer and, as the party slipped in the polls, so more and more backbenchers have slipped over to outright opposition. Surely that has to do with party politics and not the merits of the case, which have not changed.

Labour's reluctance to exploit this situation is partly due to the minority in their own party who see the European Union as a capitalist conspiracy and who believe that it prevents our planning our own way back to full employment. But it is probably governed more by the steady anti-European drumbeat in that large part of our press controlled by foreign owners, to whose quasi-monopolies the European Union is the only effective threat.

The case for retaining a British right to devalue the pound can be based only on the belief that the pound is an inherently inflationary currency. But the argument which was put forward during the 1980s for linking the pound to the then European Monetary System was based on the experience of the countries which, by linking their national currencies to the EMS, had broken that inflationary expectation. Most of them had tough trades unions and had had to concede inflationary increases year after year.

The first fight came in France in the early 1980s after the election of a Socialist government, with the usual expenditure promises. But very soon came the conflict between the election promises and the undertakings to keep the value of the franc fixed. President Mitterand decided in favour of the strong franc: the *franc fort*. From then on, the expectations were changed in both currency and labour markets. Ireland, a normally profligate country, which had put down an international airport in Mayo to win key votes, also joined. Ray MacSharry made his reputation by cutting back the expenditure to keep the Irish punt (pound) in the system. The same happened in profligate Denmark, which before then had overborrowed and always been bailed out by German banks on the basis that it was a small country and therefore a small problem.

So, it was argued, it was useless to say that we had to wait until 'the time was ripe'. So long as we stayed out, Britain would suffer from inflationary expectations. Only the commitment of membership would change these expectations as it had in every other country which had joined. Except for Mrs Thatcher, there was widespread agreement.

Mrs Thatcher lost her two Cabinet heavyweights on the issue: Geoffrey Howe, her first chancellor and Nigel Lawson, her second. It was only when her third chancellor, John Major, also insisted that at last she gave in. He probably felt that to seal the agreement quickly he had to go in on the existing sterling exchange rate, which may have been too high. But, what was more serious, it was already recognised that the EMS was too lightweight for an EU enlarged from nine to twelve and, since the Single European Act, open for free movement of goods and, more important for EMS, of currency.

It was argued that without a stronger currency system a country in trade deficit could wake up to the loss of half its currency reserves before breakfast. So the stronger European Monetary Union was proposed instead. But it was not to come into operation for nine years; meanwhile the weak EMS had to do and on Black Wednesday it was Britain which lost half its currency reserves before breakfast. At home this was seen as an indictment of the EMU; but the EMU did not yet exist and now is intended to prevent just such a crisis.

It is odd that those who are most against our membership of the EMU are those who would be most against the old instruments which governments of the 1960s and 1970s shaped to achieve full employment without inflation. Incomes policies are anathema to the monetarist, so we must assume that their main instrument to restrain inflation would be continued high unemployment and that the main instrument to keep sterling afloat would be high interest rates. If that gives a picture of an unstable and stagnant economy, then they should spell out how they see the future. To me it looks very bleak and uncertain.

Reform in the City

We have argued in the previous chapter that we should be able, at minimum cost, to remove the short-term risks and increase industrial investment substantially by improving the relationship between companies and their institutional owners. The sharp reaction of the City to Will Hutton's *The State We're In* shows how sensitive it is to criticism. And, since the confidence of the City is vital to sterling, no government likes to upset it.

It survived several investigations aimed to see whether British industry is held up by a shortage of capital. The answer has always been that there is plenty of capital and the City is always willing to invest in viable proposals. It is not the answer that is wrong, it is the question. It should be, 'Can the investment institutions improve their relations with industry to their mutual benefit?' The sub-question should be, 'If the continental countries can have closer and more productive relationships, why can we not have the same?'

It is much better to approach in a framework of mutual enquiry than to try to make them answer a hostile indictment. Despite the spread of unrestrained greed, there is a great deal of good in our financial institutions, which are still staffed by dedicated professional management, and I do not think that any change will be made unless it is matched to the old traditions of the major city institutions, which still carry great weight.

I spent a lot of energy at one time in my life in looking at the relationship between the financial institutions and industry. It is not easy for institutions to change their basic role. Any change must respect the main role of pension funds, which is to assess the life expectancy of those who look to them for pensions between retirement and death and make sure that the funds are there to meet the liability. For a long time, they matched the risks they took with investment in the bond market, in which narrow expertise they became highly skilled. With inflation and the 'cult of the equity' they became, accidentally, the major owners of British industry. It was their instinct for risk management which told them to spread the risk between as many different industries and companies as they could and to sell out at the first sign of trouble. Their main use of their accidently acquired voting rights was to make sure that the terms of new issues looked after existing shareholders. They made no attempt to second-guess the company's management and were content that boards of directors chose their new colleagues because they felt that they did not have the professional experience to interfere with them.

No one noticed, when this quiet revolution took place, that it breaches the basic social principle that power must be matched by responsibility. They need to recognise that a public company is more than just the sum total of its equity shareholders. It employs thousands of workers; it has management who may have given it their life's loyalty; it has a reputation with customers and suppliers which might be more permanent and is certainly closer than that with its shareholders. They need to acknowledge that a hostile bid is bound to be based on figures alone and will tear apart what is good as well as what is bad. It is hatchet work, when what is needed is skilled surgery.

The argument for the hostile bid is that it is the only way of dealing with sleepy and incompetent managers and of getting the best use out of the assets. In the Anglo-American system there seems to be no institutional machinery for constructive dialogue. The object of the exercise should be to see how machinery could be developed so that the pensions funds and others could arrange methods of establishing constructive and on-going dialogue and to find ways of protecting well-managed companies from hostile and disruptive bids.

Outside the British and American stock markets, the law and
the culture is in favour of matching power with responsibility,
so it is not easy in Japan or in continental Europe to make a
hostile takeover bid. The company is seen as a social as well
as an economic unit and the institutional owners take an active
interest in its long-term future. And on economic performance
the Anglo-Saxons do quite a bit worse. So it is at least worth
looking at ways in which power and responsibility could be put
back together again.

The overheating of the labour market

There is no doubt that while one part of the Treasury would
welcome the removal of hundreds of thousands of workers from
the dole queue, another part of the Treasury would worry about
the inflationary effect of an over-heated labour market, especially
a shortage of skilled labour. As we noted above, Conservative
governments have abolished the industry training boards which
levied the whole of their industry, and it is not clear whether
the TECs which took their place would have the resources to
turn out the skilled workers to the scale and standard needed
to enable industry to expand. This is not the place to go into
detail about the merits of the changes which have taken place, but
government should set up an urgent enquiry as to the numbers of
trained people of the right standard who are available and the
adequacy of the present system and the resources available for
providing what is needed.

It is also clear that a tightening of the labour market could tilt
the balance of bargaining power back towards employees. This
should not worry employers unduly, since the structural changes
which have been made in the last eighteen years make sure that
shop-floor power can no longer hold companies to ransom as it
did. But it would be well to look to the institutional arrangements
for cooperation with employees. I doubt whether the German
system of worker directors would work in Britain; but elected
works councils for companies employing more than a thousand
would create a helpful sense of partnership. It is at that size that

a sense of identity, community and joint enterprise is lost and that distrust creates unnecessary problems.

Tighter labour markets will also need a change in the culture of management. The business schools have been strong on technique, but with unemployment over two million for almost all of the last eighteen years – a whole generation of management – the labour market has been in management's favour. More people want jobs than can find them. Tight labour markets will need skills which the best managers have always exercised; in finding, training, motivating and above all keeping good people at all levels in a company. They are skills which a new generation of managers will have to learn afresh.

Can a united European effort restore full employment?

If we really want full employment, then we will not only have to learn to live with our European neighbours, but we will also have to learn how to take the initiative in the European Union to promote further joint action where we alone cannot achieve our objectives, including full employment. A British government should negotiate policies with our European partners which will help us all to get out of our present stagnation. My experience over fifteen years is that where we join our interests to our partners in the most powerful grouping in the world we are able to look after ourselves. Europe works because our interests are close to those of our near neighbours and because we need each other.

When we were looking at the further possibilities of the single European market, one which stood out was that of coordinating the economic growth of the member states. While each country had to support its currency out of its own reserves, it was inclined to let its trade grow on the coat tails of those who were growing faster. That helped their exports, but it also meant that the countries growing faster attracted a level of imports which forced them to slow down. With EMU that may not matter so much but, all the same, we need a weighty EU institution which will be as dedicated to economic growth and full employment as the new central bank will be to fighting inflation.

This growth could not be stalled, as national growth is so often stifled by currency speculation. A single European currency, with a strong central bank dedicated to the maintenance of its value, would also be able to hold its own in currency markets and would not be vulnerable to the shocks which can rock national currencies and force their governments to put on all the brakes.

The problem of poorer countries in the EU

There are genuine anxieties that EMU would make difficulties for countries which are poorer and have higher unemployment. This is a view which might properly be held by those who still believe that Keynesian growth based on government stimulation of the economy is the best way of getting people back to work – though some who are far from Keynesian have been floating it.

There is a strong consensus of opinion, with which I agree, that government stimulation was effective when government borrowing was low and the interest charges a very small part of the national budget. But, fifty years on, most democratic governments are overborrowed, interest rates are a high proportion of government expenditure and it is no longer possible for most governments, including our own, to stimulate growth by borrowing and spending.

The United States has a single currency covering states which have wide differences in unemployment rates, and the pattern there is for industry which depends on unskilled or semi-skilled labour to move to the states which have the right pool of workers and for their place in the old industrial 'rust belt' to be taken by skilled workers retrained for new high-tech industry.

This mobility of capital is possible within an area which has a single currency. It is much riskier where there is a local currency which has an uncertain exchange rate or where, if there were real economic difficulties, investors might not be able to get their money out. So countries with high unemployment, like Spain, are extremely anxious to get into the first wave of monetary union and they have good reason.

So long as the restoration of full employment seems to depend on governments' borrowing and spending, leading to the old wage–price spiral, it will not figure on the national agenda. But if it can be done by a benign package of measures, including lower interest rates based on a stable common European currency, it is in the interests of everyone except the nationalists.

THE POLITICAL ORDER

Chapter Eight

THE FRAGILITY OF FREEDOM

The old certainties are slipping

There is great reassurance in the solidity of the old buildings around Whitehall and Westminster. The Queen's standard flies from the mast on Buckingham Palace as it did for her father, grandfather, great-grandfather and great-great-grandmother Victoria, who came to the throne in 1837. The old clubs of London, founded not long after that, still stand along Pall Mall: the Athenaeum with its university vice-chancellors and bishops; the Travellers, with its ambassadors; the Reform, bastion of the cross-party Establishment; and the Oxford and Cambridge with its Whitehall mandarins and heads of colleges. Westminster Abbey has stood unscathed for nearly a thousand years, since it was founded by Edward the Confessor; and Big Ben, the symbol of the nation, has sounded its famous chimes through war and peace.

But underneath that surface all has changed. The dynamic which built those structures has long since departed. That is why we instinctively look back instead of looking forward. The past is a rosy sunset, the future is black obscurity. What we look at today are the symbols of a system which no longer works. We go through the same rituals, but they do not represent today's reality. And, as we try to come to grips with the present reality, we fumble.

Our very riches make us vulnerable. We are geared to high output and high consumption, which we have achieved by a degree of specialisation never before known. The great slump of the thirties was more tolerable because most industrial countries still had a large rural, agricultural base and there were urban craftsmen who could use their own skill to make a saleable product. Homes were not mechanised and there was a huge market for domestic labour.

Today all that has changed. We are far more mechanised and much more highly organised and very few people can make their way on their own. If they are not working for an organisation, the chances of their earning a living are slender. Such people are outside the economic system and have no stake in or loyalty to the political system which has excluded them.

The other change is that in all societies until now, the family has felt responsible for those of its members who needed help. This is still true today in Asian and African societies, and used also to be true in Europe. But family solidarity is now becoming a thing of the past and those who are out of the economic system are likely to find themselves out of the social system too.

The welfare state at risk

The welfare state is now under severe pressure. All the talk is of cuts in social benefit, because the welfare system was not meant to bear the permanent burden of paying two million people to do nothing. The break up of the family has cut the number of new births and, not too far ahead, that will reduce the number of earners whose tax is needed to pay the pensions of those who have retired. This is yet another heavy burden on the budget not foreseen by the architects of the welfare state, who were dealing in their day with a buoyant rise in population.

The welfare state also supposed that government could tax the rich to help the poor as, until the 1970s, it still did. Tax cuts in the 1980s were paid for by the bonus of North Sea oil and by selling off the state investments. Since then government has had to borrow heavily, but it cannot keep up this level for ever without great damage to the investment needed for jobs. Also the willingness of those who are earning to pay for those who are not is rapidly diminishing. That shows in the reluctance of government and opposition to talk about tax increases, but it also shows in the rise in tax avoidance and, perhaps, with the recent fall in expected VAT, in tax evasion.

With only 2 per cent of the world's population and very limited natural resources Britain has incomes which are ten times the world's average. To keep that up we have to live on our wits, to make the best of our ability to invent and make new products and to sell enough goods and services to pay for our imports of raw materials. We live on the narrow edge between economic success and failure so we have to make the most of our trading advantages, and we cannot afford major disruptions to our highly geared industrial and commercial system. Yet, if we keep two million people out of the system for much longer, we are making ourselves very vulnerable to those who think they have more to gain than lose by smashing the system in order to bring themselves forcibly to our attention.

English nationalism

Our economy is also vulnerable to the rising tide of English nationalism, which could too easily draw in a backlash of racialism. Half a century after the last nationalist war, in which Europe lost thirty-five million dead, nationalism is again coming into fashion. There are nationalist parties in France, Germany, Austria and Belgium; nationalism has torn Yugoslavia apart and recreated ten or more tiny republics in Eastern Europe. Above all there is now a large section of the British Conservative Party who are quite prepared to split the party and lose the next election for the cause of English nationalism.

All this would also do the greatest damage to our social cohesion, to democracy and to the tolerance of which we have always been so proud. The question is whether our political system is strong enough to deal with the challenge.

Change needs to be conducted on agreed principles

The success of any social system – indeed of any system – depends on its flexibility in adapting to change. And flexibility, in turn, depends on a sound set of basic principles. It is they which tell us how to adapt and how to rebuild for the future and it is those basic principles which we have now lost. So we each cling on obstinately to separate bits of our heritage, which no longer fit into a functioning whole.

Parliament insists on the sovereignty it no longer exercises; governments assure us that it is still quite all right to govern with the majority of the electorate against them and that they do not have to act even when found by committees of enquiry to be in the wrong. Despite the long list of scandals, many financial institutions believe that the freer the market the better. Despite the unprecedented break up of the family, the intellectuals assure us that we are happier that way. And despite the huge rise in crimes of violence, we are told that it is just part of a cycle and that the number of attacks will drop off again in due course.

The man and woman in the street, not believing any of this, look round for a scapegoat: immigrants, Brussels, politicians, or violence on TV. Or they pick some issue on which to crusade and try to put one bit of the world right all on their own. Or they opt out and go in for transcendental meditation or New Age beliefs.

The trouble is that general principles, however vital, do not have such a powerful lobby as existing interests. Take the key issue as to whether it is right to govern with 'conviction politics' when the majority of the country is against you. Both government and opposition have a vested interest and so do most MPs in both the major parties. It needs a very strong belief in principle to rouse the country to see that this is not only undemocratic but dangerous. Those in power not only have the ability to keep the system as it is, they also command the government propaganda machine. And, since there is a consensus of the main parties, the iniquity of the system never gets a hearing.

Political reform

Yet there were times when the iniquity of minority rule was changed against the interests of those who held it. Absolute monarchy, despite the restoration of Charles II, never recovered from the Puritans. Oligarchical government gave way in 1832, when the influence of the Methodists had penetrated to the upper classes. The second Reform Bill of 1867, which brought a huge expansion of the franchise, came after the great religious revival of 1859. By the end of the century the Christian idealism had faded and the goodwill of those in power was not enough to solve the Irish problem, despite the most powerful efforts of the greatest political orator of the day, William Gladstone. And women's franchise probably had more to do with the need for women in industry in World War I than with the suffragettes' impressive campaign for votes for women.

Changes of government do give a large part of the minority a turn in power, but eighteen years of one-party government have alienated great sections of the country and dangerously undermined the legitimacy of democratic government. This might not have mattered so much had there been an elected second chamber in Parliament or a strong tier of local government. But in eighteen years the local governments, which are nearer to the people and command strong local loyalties, have been stripped both of money and of power.

National government had argued that too many large cities had had one-party government for too long, that power had been abused, and that job-creating industry and commerce had been driven out by excessively high local rates. So rates were capped and the financial powers of elected councillors cut back until they could no longer look after the interests of the citizens who elected them. This was very damaging for the ideals of democracy. The largest local government, the Greater London Council, was simply wound up and County Hall sold off.

Most other countries, with the same problem of one-party domination of cities and counties, have found the answer in making the local government tier cover a much wider area. In the United States, Canada, Australia, Spain, Germany and Italy there are regional governments. Though much larger than our city or county councils, these tap the local loyalty of the Californians, the British Columbians, the Western Australians, the Bavarians, the Catalans, and the Lombards and they make people feel a lot nearer to their elected representatives, without running the same risk of perpetual one-party rule.

It would make a lot of sense to have regional government elected by the peoples of Wales and Scotland, and of Yorkshire, Lancashire and other English regions. There is already a real sense of identity and the regional capitals would have some sense of power, of including their own key figures in worthwhile decision-making. But the idea is bitterly opposed because it would undermine the power of Westminster and Whitehall. Meanwhile the number of people alienated from the democratic system has been greatly increased by the cutting down of their local government.

Ethnic minorities

Democratic government depends on the acceptance by the minority of government by the majority. In Britain today we have the added complication of very substantial ethnic minorities. The first were the Irish. De Valéra's nationalism had the perverse effect of driving a great many more Irish to England to earn their living. The saying in the pubs of Dublin was, 'They told us that there would be more jobs after the election; what they didn't tell us was that they would all be in Birmingham.' There now are probably a million Irish in England and, since violence in Northern Ireland, but more especially since the bombings in England, they have felt increasingly separate and vulnerable. A number of unsafe convictions for terrorism have not helped.

There are certainly a million Muslims, with heavy concentrations in a few places, but spread throughout the country. There are also a great many non-Muslim Indians – mainly Sikhs – and a long tail from other Asian countries – Vietnamese and overseas Chinese. There are the old and relatively small Jewish community, the huge numbers of West Indians and the less distinct American- and European-born citizens and residents.

Ethnic minorities need a stable, self-confident social order. But the pub talk is that if we didn't have two million immigrants there would not be two million unemployed. Sixty years ago the Jews in Germany were of long descent and well integrated into the social order at every level. Our immigrants are new and so, if there were any collapse of order, they could be extremely vulnerable. Nor are they all the same. There is a high proportion of blacks among the unemployed and a rising number among young Asians. But a great many Asians make their living in corner shops which otherwise would have closed down. The most enterprising Asians have set up their own businesses and created new employment. But mob oratory would grind these subtleties to powder.

The white male manual worker who has been accustomed to a steady job feels the loss most acutely. The unemployed man with a wife out at work feels especially useless. In a TV programme on the valleys of South Wales, a group of unmarried mothers agreed that they saw no use for men. The one man in camera sat sheepishly in a corner. A backlash would no doubt sweep political correctness aside in an effort to put that right too.

The danger of a nationalist backlash

The unemployed could not engineer a backlash on their own. They might challenge the police for control of the streets, but only if they were organised. They would need the help of those who were used to power and resented its loss.

The argument in soundbites in front of the TV cameras also helps those who want the debate to be conducted in slogans, and there is no time to follow through with the 'yes, but' or the 'what about?'

We moved in the nationalist direction when, following the British government's announcement about BSE, the German, Italian and

French farmers lost nearly half their domestic customers, whom they could only begin to recover by banning British beef. The English nationalists, ignoring the crisis which we ourselves had created for continental farmers and governments, forced the British government to bring all European business to a halt until their stricken markets were once more open to the small exports of British beef. That did enormous damage to the major British interests, which the ultimate government fudge could not recover. But the Union Jacks being burnt by German farmers could only help the nationalist case by creating a new hostility to back their dogma that the hostility had been there all along. Patriots try to make friends for their country, but nationalism needs enemies.

For me that was the last straw, the moment when strong loyalty to the hundreds of constituency workers who had supported me for fifteen years was no longer enough. For those years it had been my job to protect the real British interest in Europe and those who cared nothing for that had been allowed to do it irreparable harm. I could no longer support a party so dominated by nationalists.

Over those years I had learned that the only way to look after British interests was to identify our major interests with those of our partners. Time and again, in the reform of the Common Agricultural Policy (CAP), in the creation of the Single Market and in a hundred lesser policies, we had put together a parliamentary majority which had carried the British interest. In the years before I was an MEP, when I was a British public servant, I had learned that in almost everything which ultimately mattered in defence, finance and trade, Britain could not get its way alone. We needed friends. We are now told by those who have never had to negotiate for the national interest that all we have to do is to insist in a loud voice and it will be done. We used to have a colleague in the European Parliament, an ex-MP, who told us what to say 'to these foreigners'. Our reply was that he should talk to them himself. Then there were boundary changes and he had to submit himself for re-selection. The perceptive selection committee turned him down on the grounds that, even after five years, he did not seem to know enough about Europe!

Yet the anti-European drumbeat of the tabloids shows that the new nationalist rhetoric has a good deal of resonance. It may be that this is because no British government, since Edward Heath lost office in 1974, has put the positive case for partnership with our European neighbours. Since Mrs Thatcher's Bruges speech in 1988 created the illusion of a hostile Europe, almost all the rhetoric has been hostile. It is also certainly because the 60 per cent of the British national press which is foreign-owned has its own commercial reasons for being hostile, and will not publish any letters or articles which go against its usual line.

But none of this would matter if there were not a strong nationalist sentiment among the general public. There is a broad constituency on which a new English nationalist party could draw. Even though the Labour Party and union leaders now see the strong economic interests in British membership of the European Union, there is nationalist feeling in the pubs and working men's clubs. But it is also strong among those in the political class who do not speak another language, who do not have the European connections of business and trades unions, whose political contacts are in Whitehall and Westminster and who feel sidelined by decision-making outside these familiar haunts. This group would include most political journalists, whose working capital is bound in the Filofax with the phone numbers of their contacts, almost all of them British.

In the business community, anti-European feeling includes those whose ideology is right-wing and the thousands of small businesses who do not have any foreign customers, who are represented by the Institute of Directors, rather than by those who have to deal with our vital export trade, the CBI or the Chambers of Commerce. They also represent the kind of business which is labour-intensive, and so they are exceptionally sensitive to European proposals for the protection of workers from excessive hours and the setting of safe working standards and minimum wages.

There is also a great army of retired colonels and some headmasters, who write from quaint villages in the west of England and who believe that our national identity is at stake. Harold Wilson, a British prime minister who won four elections, was according to *Spycatcher* kept under surveillance because of doubts about some of his foreign connections. But we have been extremely fortunate that, since John Churchill (later the first Duke of Marlborough) left his command of King James' army by night to desert to William of Orange, the British armed forces have kept out of politics.

But there are certainly professing Christians who are, on principle, against the European Union and would also be behind any attempt to bring back moral and social order, even if this were at some cost to democracy. There are also Christians who see the European Union as a Catholic plot. Many identify it with the antichrist of the book of Revelation and the refounding of the Roman Empire, and see the monarch's coronation oath as a protection against the power of the Roman Catholic church. This view is most explicitly held by Dr Ian Paisley, MP, but also by a far broader group of Ulster Unionists and by many in England too, where it goes with nineteenth-century dispensational theology.

The political philosophy which could hold all these disparate groups together is nationalism. Nationalism makes loyalty to your own folk into a religion for which all believers have to fight. We have seen what Irish nationalism has done to the British Isles and how hard it is for a sovereign Irish government to put the genie of nationalism back in the bottle, even after nearly thirty years of strife in Northern Ireland. We have seen too how easy it is for Irish nationalism to create the same intractable spirit even among those who call themselves unionists and loyalists.

Already we have Welsh and Scottish nationalism, kept in check by a socialism which reaches out across frontiers to all workers. But were socialism to fail, and were English nationalism to take root as the alternative political force, then there is no doubt which alternative the Scots and Welsh would choose. The United Kingdom would break up.

We should not be surprised at the rise of English nationalism. Nationalism comes to countries which have lost their self-confidence, who have lost a former greatness and authority and feel a need to reassert themselves.

It is not easy for any country to see their own nationalism for what it is. The spirit of the age (what the Germans call the Zeitgeist) is invisible to those who live with it. It is just what everyone believes, isn't it? It is what the British tabloids say about the French and the Germans. It is shown in its crudest form by the behaviour which caused the expulsion of the English football teams from the continent. What seems to us to be just a joke or youthful high spirits looks very different to those on the receiving end.

At the receiving end, they see clearly the virus of nationalism. They tell their British friends and colleagues about the Germans who say, 'If the British can be nationalistic, why can't we?' There are now nearly ninety million Germans and a united Germany, which has dominated the continent twice before and has sworn that it will never do so again. But sometimes we make it hard for a German government which faces an opposition party tempted to whip up public opinion against the tolerance of their rulers.

If the next government were determined to make Britain a leading partner in the European Union, that would give us a breathing space for four years or more. But were it to fail, we could have a right-wing backlash in the shape of an English nationalist government, coming to power on as little as 38 per cent of the votes – maybe even less.

In 1933 the Nazis came to power in Germany, quite legally, on a minority of votes. They got enough support from other right-wing parties to form a government and together they persuaded an aged President Hindenburg to appoint Adolf Hitler as Chancellor. Hitler also overcame the resistance of the regional governments and persuaded the army that he would look after their interests.

We share enough of the background of Germany in the early thirties to worry. The Germans had lost an empire; so have we. They felt that they were a great nation, shunted unfairly on to the sidelines; so do we. The Germans felt that they were surrounded by enemies; we are busily persuading ourselves of the same. The traditional German was outraged at the loose morals of the Weimar Republic and the decadence of Berlin; a lot of people in Britain today would echo that feeling. The Germans were suffering from prolonged high unemployment; ours is not quite so bad, but half the German population was on the land, which eased their problem. Unemployment in a wholly urban country is, as pointed out earlier, far worse. Their inflation had been worse than ours, but the worst was over and so for the moment is ours. Yet the German family was holding together as ours is not and the morals of the Weimar Republic have nothing on the morals of Britain today, so there is not enough difference to assure us that it could never happen here. And for a scapegoat, substitute the recent immigrants to Britain for the far less obvious indigenous Jews in Germany.

Constitutionally an English nationalist party would have a much easier ride. With our voting system, they would not have to look for coalition partners. President Hindenburg's great prestige and the German constitution would have allowed him to refuse Hitler. Under our unwritten constitution, our monarch could not refuse to call on the leader of the party with the largest number of votes in the House of Commons to form a government. In Britain there is no entrenched local government which could stand in the way of an elected national government, as there was in Germany. And Hitler had to worry about the army while the strong tradition of the British armed forces is against interference in politics.

Once Hitler was Chancellor and with the Interior Ministry and police in his hands, he invented a crisis – the Reichstag fire – introduced emergency rule and ruled without parliamentary opposition. By then, as the majority of Germans found, it was too late. A British nationalist government would not find it any more difficult to introduce emergency rule with or without a crisis.

Nationalism in Europe

For forty-five years after the war, nationalism was banished from Europe. The European Economic Community was set up to make sure that differences were settled by debate and not by bombs. With the exception of three small countries – Iceland, Norway and Switzerland – all of Western Europe are now members and the Central European countries have applied to join and are already members of the Council of Europe.

In Eastern Europe and the Balkans, communism took over and national differences were suppressed by force. Now that communism has disappeared, nationalism is out again in full force. It is at its worst in the former republic of Yugoslavia, where people who had lived together peacefully – save for the war – since 1919, have suddenly gone for each other's throats. The reason is not insanity but, as in Northern Ireland, the fear which nationalism arouses. Because the safeguards of the multinational state have been removed, yesterday's friend may be today's enemy and either you strike first or he does. In Northern Ireland there are two minorities: the nationalists in Northern Ireland and the unionists in the island of Ireland. Once violence starts, even for a good cause, it is very hard to stop it without a fight to the finish, which the British government is still able to prevent – though the sudden switch of tactics at Drumcree in July 1996 showed how fine is the line between law and order and mob rule.

Nationalism is not the same as patriotism. Nationalism needs enemies. If it does not have them, it invents them, as Mrs Thatcher invented them in her 1988 Bruges speech, giving licence to others to go far further than she did. Patriotism tries to settle differences in the interests of both parties in order to maintain good relations; nationalism stirs up differences to create solidarity against the outsider. Patriotism tries to keep the peace; nationalism leads inexorably to violence. Patriotism is tolerant of different views within the commonwealth; nationalism is always looking for enemies within. Patriotism protects democracy; but nationalism leads to one-party 'government of national unity'.

There may be those who think that this could not happen in England, but the changes in our moral and social structure in the last thirty years are unprecedented. We are in uncharted waters. Britain may have suffered violence in the past, but our complex industrial economy now makes us so dependent on each other and on our trading partners that our capacity to tolerate violence without catastrophic disruption is now very small. Villages and towns used to be self-sufficient; local farms looked after local markets. Local craftsmen could put right most of what went wrong. Neighbours looked after each other without need of an organised police. Not any more. Two men with a bomb can close down a city centre and no one can get to work. Roadblocks could empty the supermarkets in a few days.

So the level of violence which can make the people call for strong government and emergency rule is a lot lower today than it was even in Hitler's Germany. We may find that though we want democracy, a majority want order first. Dictators around the world always promise that when order is restored, we can have democratic elections again. But, for one plausible reason or another, it seldom happens.

The church against the backlash?

I do not see how the present intellectual élite can stand in the way of such a populist, nationalist reaction. They are not organised throughout the country as the church is. They do not command the loyalty which the church commands. They are composed of writers, journalists and broadcasters, but the only part of their agenda which the public have accepted is that they can do things now which were not allowed before. But that is the easy part. Standing in the way of a massive panic at the disappearance of public order is, I think, beyond them. Post-modernism with all its doubts will be swept away. People will want certainty, even if it is wrong.

It is to the shame of the German church in 1933 that it did not stand against Hitler. The reason was that it was riddled with a liberalism which had removed the absolutes of right and wrong, the certainty of Christian truth. Having removed the foundations, it could not stand up against the storm. Those sections of the church in Britain which went in the same direction are now represented by empty pews. It is that part of the church which stands for the age-old certainties of the Christian faith which remain strong and which will have to stand the strain if and when the backlash comes. We are taught to stand firm even if it means martyrdom. And our points of resistance are quite clear.

The Christian faith teaches that, in God's kingdom, there is neither 'Jew nor Gentile, Barbarian or Scythian, all are one in Christ Jesus'. Men and women from every race and class are created in the image of God. So, in the Christian church above all, there is to be no racial barrier. It was when, at last, they applied that teaching, that the Dutch Orthodox Church opened the way for a peaceful transfer of power in South Africa. It took long years of painful argument, but in the end it was done. It was the prior unity of the Christian church which produced one kingdom out of all the Anglo-Saxon tribes.

Since Christians believe in the unity of the human race, they do not believe, as the Nazis did, in *untermenschen* – people who were beneath regard. So every citizen has the same rights, regardless of origin. We cannot discriminate. Hitler believed that only the fittest should survive and that the power of the fit could be used against the unfit. He had no difficulty with euthanasia. The Christian believes that God counts the hairs on every head and that men and women, disabled, babies, feeble and aged are precious. We are not the same as animals. On all these issues the Christian is bound to dig in and resist.

Absolute rulers have always regarded the Christian church with the deepest suspicion. They do not mind too much the rituals of church services, so long as the churches are registered and confine themselves to worship. But they dare not allow freedom of the pulpit to those who have a network of dedicated people all across the country, who meet at least once a week and have an uncensored platform for their leaders. Who else is organised at city, regional and national level and, above all, who else has a loyalty which is superior to their loyalty to the state?

History proves the suspicious rulers right. The early church survived the Roman Empire despite the persecutions. The church in Greece survived the long Turkish occupation; the churches in Central and Eastern Europe have survived the Communist empire. Even in Communist China, the Christian church is now estimated at fifty million – the largest in the world. So, even in human terms there is a power which has been shown to be capable of resisting evil.

But it would be much better if the churches used that power to make sure that the evil did not arrive, if we bent all our efforts to the reforms which are needed in society to remove the causes of moral and social collapse. We should do all we can to relieve the suffering so that the church earns respect as the early church earned respect, by being a good neighbour to those in need. And, if we do all that, we will have a good deal more support for the lines we try to draw between right and wrong, when evil people attempt to remove the liberties of the citizen.

The price of democracy is eternal vigilance. So, even if we think it unlikely that the thousands of young unemployed can be transformed into Brownshirts who take over the streets and enforce their own version of order; we should do what we can to make sure that it never comes to that.

Chapter Nine

Britain's guiding light

What makes our national identity?

There is a great deal of heated talk today about preserving Britain's national identity, making sure that it is not melted down in some European porridge. The former French President, Valéry Giscard-d'Estaing, once came to speak in Cambridge and told his audience that we should not worry too much about the imagined danger of losing our national identity. 'We old countries, Britain and France, we understand each other. I will always be a Frenchman; you could not imagine anything else. And you too, you will always be British. You would not wish me to be any different and I could not wish you to be any different.' Manuel Fraga, the founder of the present government party in Spain, said something similar in a speech in the European Parliament. 'No one could accuse me of not being a patriotic Spaniard. I am and always will be a Spaniard, but I am also a European and I do not see any conflict.'

England and Scotland are even older than France and Spain – and Wales is older than both – but what *is* our national identity? What are the common threads which have made us, without doubt, a leading nation in the world? What is it exactly that we need to preserve? What is the warp and woof of a nation's social fabric? What inspires its people from one generation to another? What were the foundations of our laws and customs? To answer all that we need to go back to the beginning and then trace these threads through the centuries.

The fifth and sixth centuries – after the Romans left and before the Angles, Saxons and Jutes formed themselves into a nation – are the 'dark ages' of which we do not have much certain record. Only in the seventh century, when the Roman church sent Augustine to convert the pagan invaders, do we begin to have a written history, mostly written by Bede.

Augustine got as far as Canterbury, but he did not last long and it was only when another Roman, Theodore, came that one tribal king after another converted from paganism to Christianity and bishops were consecrated across England. Stenton in his *Anglo-Saxon England* puts the council held at Hertford in 672 as the 'definite stage in the process which wore down the separatism of the different English kingdoms'. The last to be converted were the South Saxons and then all England was united in the Christian faith.

We do not know the motives of the kings in accepting Christianity. It may have been a political act rather than an act of faith; but, whatever the origins, it soon became popular. Stenton says, 'The monastic ideal influenced the whole character of the early Christian church for its first century.' The conversion of the invading pagans in northern Europe was also influenced by the dedication of the simple Christian monastic missions which were planted among the pagan tribes, where they showed an unselfish care for the people to whom they were sent, which shone in marked contrast to the society around them. So, though they had to have the permission or formal 'conversion' of the tribal chief, what made the faith stick and the pagan beliefs wither was its popularity and acceptance among ordinary people.

The church unites the nation

So England was united by its church before it was united as a kingdom. It was not long before the newly Christian Anglo-Saxons were put to the test by the attacks of the Vikings, as pagan as the Anglo-Saxons had been before them. The key figure was Alfred, who succeeded his brother as king of Wessex and who, by recapturing London from the Danes, was acknowledged as first among the Anglo-Saxon kings and is rightly regarded today as the first king of England. Finally the Danes came to terms. They retained the Danelaw of East Anglia and were themselves converted to the Christian faith. Through intermarriage they eventually succeeded Alfred's weakening dynasty as kings of England. Apart from Harald's brief reign in 1066, the last successor to King Cnut was Edward the Confessor, a saintly figure who founded Westminster Abbey.

For its first three or four hundred years in England, the Christian church seems to have been far nearer to the early church than to the increasing riches, grandeur and power which followed in the four and a half centuries down to the Reformation. It was some time before the monastic missions and field churches round simple crosses developed into settled parishes, each with its minister. The original churches were wooden and thatched and those Saxon churches which survive – there is one in Cambridge on the Newmarket Road – are small and simple. The bishop was a key figure and he had to teach and preach as well as to organise and adjudicate.

Though there was only a century between the conversion of the Roman Emperor Constantine and the collapse of Roman rule in Britain, there were some Christians among the ancient Britons who were driven by the Saxons into Wales. It was from Wales that St Patrick went to convert the Irish; from Ireland that St Columba came to convert the Scots; and from Scotland that missionaries came to the Anglo-Saxon invaders of northern England. The Celtic church in northern England and the Roman-founded church in southern England were joined at the Synod of Whitby in 663. To complete the story of the missionary journeys, it was from England that Boniface went in 716, first to Frisia on the Dutch coast, then to Hesse and Thuringia in Germany on the borders of the kingdom of the Franks, where, with the help of numerous Englishmen, he founded many churches and was appointed archbishop, taking Mainz as his see. Eventually he was given the task of reforming the church of the powerful Frankish kingdom, which stretched from central Germany to the Pyrenees.

The church is corrupted by power and money

In the three centuries after the Norman conquest, and as Western Europe became settled under its new rulers, the Christian church became rich and powerful and subject to the corruptions which riches and power bring with them. Much of its behaviour in the centuries between the crusades and the Borgia popes is not defensible on any interpretation of the teaching of Christ and the apostles.

The crusades against Islam, launched under papal blessing, cannot be justified by a faith whose founder said that 'the meek shall inherit the earth' and who told the apostle Peter to put away his sword. Even today, centuries later, Muslims complain about the unprovoked aggression of Christianity, an aggression fully repaid by the Ottoman attacks on Europe and the occupation of the Balkans for five centuries.

In the late Middle Ages, not only were the functions of church and state confused, but the princes wanted some of the power of the church for themselves. These were the years of the German prince–bishops; the time when the English king, Henry II, appointed a favourite courtier as Archbishop of Canterbury, found him unexpectedly defending the power of the church against the state and asked his knights, 'Who will rid me of this turbulent priest?' It was on a pilgrimage to the tomb of the martyred Thomas à Becket that Chaucer set his *Canterbury Tales* at the close of the fourteenth century.

Wyclif and the Lollards

By then the Black Death had brought a terrible judgment on that corrupt society, wiping out half the population of England in three awful visitations. And by then the first English reformer, Wyclif, had inspired the Lollard movement in the church. Chaucer contrasts the simple Lollard parson with the others who lived off the riches of the medieval church.

A Monk there was, one of the finest sort,
Who rode the country, hunting was his sport,
He let go by the things of yesterday,
And took the world's more spacious way,
Hunting a hare, or riding at a fence,
Was all his fun, he spared for no expense.

There was a Friar, a wanton one and merry,
A Limiter, a very festive fellow,
Highly beloved and intimate was he
With county folk within his boundary,
And city dames of honour and possessions,
For he was qualified to hear confessions,
Therefore instead of weeping and of prayer
One should give silver for a poor Friar's care.

There was a Summoner with us at that Inn
His face on fire like a Cherubin,
Why, he'll allow – just for a quart of wine –
Any good lad to keep a concubine,
Thus as he pleased, the man could bring duress
On any young fellow in the diocese.

But he treats the Lollard parson with great respect:

A holy-minded man of good renown
And poor, the parson to a town,
Yet he was rich in holy thought and work
He also was a learned man, a clerk,
Who truly knew Christ's gospel and would preach it.
This noble example to his sheep he gave
That first he wrought and afterward he taught.
His business was to show a fair behaviour
And draw men thus to heaven and their Saviour.

The Reformation and its political consequences

The Reformation did not come for over a century, but in the intervening fifteenth century, the heirs of the Normans wiped each other out in the prolonged Wars of the Roses. After the Battle of Bosworth the throne was taken by a careful Welshman, Henry Tudor, whose father had married into the royal line, giving him enough legitimacy to back his military success. His son, Henry VIII, did not intend England to become part of Luther's Reformation but, in falling out with the Pope over a divorce from his first wife, he set in motion unstoppable forces. By the time his daughter Elizabeth came to the throne, the reformation of the Church of England had developed widespread popular support and England was now the largest Protestant country in Europe. Such was the popular support for reform in Scotland that its Catholic queen was driven out and a regent for her infant son took over power and appointed a Protestant council.

It took another hundred years to work out the implications of the Reformation in the thought and life of these two nations. Christians now had the words of Christ and the apostles in their own language and the two Reformers – Luther, and especially John Calvin – had begun to work out a reformed theology, which depended above all on the Christian and apostolic teachings and – only where they clearly agreed with those – on the traditions of the medieval church.

The Reformers taught 'the priesthood of all believers', that each Christian is responsible directly to God, to whom we should pray through Christ Jesus and not through any human priest. Christ had taught that earthly rank did not count in his kingdom where 'the first shall be last and the last first'. Before God, all men and women were equal.

It was not long before there were those who taught that authority in the church should be from the bottom up and not from the top down – which was the issue in the first civil war – and questioned whether there should be a hierarchy at all, which was the issue between Scots Presbyterians and English Independents in the second civil war. Cromwell, who was an Independent, drew the line at the proposals of the Levellers, who wanted to follow this logic straight on to political democracy; but the seed had been sown which was eventually to bear fruit; for it was in these years that attitudes to the dignity of the individual were born in British society. These have influenced us ever since.

Although the monarchy was restored in 1660, there was a further revolution twenty-eight years later, when it was established that parliament could choose the head of state. The parliamentary leaders offered the throne to the king's daughter, Mary, and her Dutch husband, William of Orange. They shared the monarchy until Mary's death, when William, who was not in the hereditary line, reigned alone.

On the death of his successor, Mary's sister Anne, the parliamentary leaders offered the throne to a distant descendant of James I: George, King of Hanover, who could not even speak English. Earlier in this century, the British prime minister, Stanley Baldwin, forced the abdication of King Edward VIII, who had insisted on marrying a divorced woman, and the throne passed to his more reliable and happily married brother Albert, who became George VI. There was no written constitution, but it was clear that the wishes of the people's representatives were supreme.

If the seventeenth-century state did not see the need to agree a written constitution, the leaders of the Presbyterian and Independent churches did. They needed to have an agreed document for their churches in place of the pronouncements of the councils of the Catholic church, one which gave more depth than the Thirty-nine Articles of the reformed Church of England. The result was the Westminster Confession, the seminal document of the English and Scots reformers at the height of their influence. It showed how all the great doctrines of the Christian faith supported, explained and balanced each other. It is a classic document of church history, has had immense influence in the whole of the English speaking world and has stood the test of time.

The Christian roots of the scientific method

The Reformation ripped away all the paraphernalia which the medieval church had put between man and God. It reintroduced the teaching of the great Augustine, fourth-century Bishop of Hippo, on the sovereignty of God. Once more Christians had to look at the nature of God and the world which he had created. They had begun to study the Bible as the book of God's word and they now began, with similar respect, to study nature as the book of God's works.

Professor Herbert Butterfield, former regius professor of history at Cambridge, regarded the emergence of the new scientific civilisation in the later seventeenth century as the greatest landmark since the rise of Christianity. In his book, *The Origins of Modern Science* (G. Bell, 1957), he says:

> Before the seventeenth century had opened, the general state of knowledge in regard to the physical universe had been conducive to the production of a number of speculative systems . . . not founded upon general enquiry, but generally compounded out of ingredients taken from classical antiquity . . . The principal leaders in this seventeenth century movement were Francis Bacon in the first quarter of the century . . . and Descartes, whose work belongs chiefly to the second quarter and who differed from Bacon in the emphasis which he placed on the deductive and philosophical method of reasoning.

The only time I ever met Harold Macmillan, he explained to me the difference between the English (Baconian) and the French (Cartesian) methods of reasoning, 'The French always have to start off with a general principle and we start off by asking whether it will work. If it will not work, we will not do it even if in principle it should work and if it does work we will do it, even if the principle says that it shouldn't.' In science, it was the pragmatic English Baconian method which won out. Christopher Hill, in his *Intellectual Origins of the English Revolution* (Oxford University Press, 1965), quotes Bacon, 'Whether knowledge is possible or not is settled not by argument, but by trying.' The scientific method, as it developed, was based on practical experiment. What could be measured, counted and tested was science, what could not was speculation.

Hill says,

In the eighty years before 1640, England, from being a
backward country in science, became one of the most
advanced ... It is no coincidence that many of the early
scientists were keen Protestants ... Rejection of the miracle
of the mass and of wonder-working images, scepticism of
all miracles since the age of the primitive church, anxiety to
minimise the area in which [Divine] intervention prevailed
and to proclaim the rule of law in the universe ... helped
to create an atmosphere favourable to science ... Galileo
was forced to recant and his ideas could be developed only
in Protestant countries ... Before Bacon began to write, the
utilitarian value of science as a means of relief for man's
estate on earth was being glorified.

Bacon was the political thinker which the movement needed.
Hill again:

Bacon gave a cooperative programme and a sense of purpose
to merchants, artisans and philosophers; he settled with
religion and established that scientific investigation did not
conflict with divinity, but was positively virtuous. Bacon elevated to a coherent intellectual system what had hitherto been
the only partial assumptions of practical men ... What Bacon
did was to join the [contemporary] scientific traditions and the
Puritan tradition and to make of them an intellectual system.

Negatively, Bacon destroyed the attachment of the church to the
teachings of Aristotle and the schoolmen. Bacon says, 'Such
teachings tend to curtail human power over nature and to
produce a deliberate and artificial despair. This despair, in its
turn confounds the promptings of hope, cuts the strings and
sinews of industry and makes men unwilling to put anything to
the hazard of trial.'

But to understand just why the scientific method sprang from
the Puritans and why it is in such danger today, we need to
understand the creed which was spelt out by the Westminster
Assembly in their great Confession.

First, unlike pagan religions, they believed in one God, who
had created the whole natural order. So what was discovered in

one part of the world would be true in another. This unity in the natural order is an essential foundation of experimental science. Second, the Bible taught that the Creator was a God of order, who had made everything 'after its kind', and who had asked the first man to classify all the animals; so nature could be analysed and classified and everything we saw would fit into an orderly pattern. We only needed to find it.

Third, the Bible taught that God was a God of reason. He reasoned with men and women, he argued that whatever they did had predictable consequences and illustrated this from the laws of nature. So there would be a rationality in the natural laws, to be discovered by all those who tried to find them out. Science was not only about classifications, but about systems – biological, ecological, geological and astronomical systems. Fourth, the Bible gave God's promise that after the last great natural catastrophe, Noah's flood, the natural laws would be stable until the end of time. God's covenant with Noah after the flood stated specifically,

> Never again will I destroy all living creatures,
>   as I have done.
> As long as the earth endures,
> seedtime and harvest,
> cold and heat,
> summer and winter,
> day and night
> will never cease. (Gen. 8:22)

Without this belief in stable natural laws, systematic scientific enquiry is not worthwhile, since what we find today may, quite arbitrarily, be changed tomorrow.

Fifth, the Bible taught that nature had been given to men and women in trust for their good. So we should try to understand the uses of all the plants and animals which God had given us. Nature, though damaged by the rebellion of the first man and woman and their descendants, was benign. Studying nature was not a pointless exercise. The fruits of nature were there for our use, if we took the trouble to look into them. It was, as Bacon put it, 'For the relief of man's estate'.

Sixth, God, who had created nature, was the great primary cause, and we, his creatures, can only understand him and his works so far as he has revealed them. So science must be about secondary causes. To be useful, science must be decoupled from speculation. In our time, the late Professor Popper expressed this as the rule that if a proposition cannot be falsified, then it is not science but metaphysics.

This separation of science from speculation was critical for the success not only of the new science, but also for the rule of law. Says Christopher Hill,

> Bacon's emphasis on secondary causes and his relegation of divine intervention to a long-past historic epoch – this fortified and gave deeper significance to the Parliamentarian preference for the rule of law . . . A similar emphasis on the law-abiding nature of the universe can be seen in the dominant school of Puritan theologians, Preston and Ames.

Britain was not alone in the development of the new scientific method. Butterfield refers to it as a shuttle of ideas between England, Holland and the French Hugenots, which, during the Thirty Years War in Germany, was the Protestant heartland. But there seems little doubt that London was in the lead.

The result has been an explosion of knowledge in three centuries such as the world has never seen in all the millennia before. But had it not been allied to what is commonly known as the Protestant ethic, the torrent of knowledge might simply have run into the sands.

The Protestant ethic

The key to the Protestant ethic is the doctrine of the 'calling'. The reformers not only taught that God knew each one of his human creatures, but also that he had given a specific calling to those who had faith in Christ's redemption and accepted his sovereignty in their lives. Salvation was, as the apostles had taught, by faith in Christ and not by the multiplication of good works; but those who professed to be Christian should show their faith by their actions. As James said in his epistle, 'Faith by itself, if it is not accompanied by action, is dead' (Jas. 2:17).

Christ taught that the first commandment was that we should love God with all our heart, mind, soul and strength, but the second was like it, to love our neighbour as ourself. When asked who was our neighbour, he preached the parable of the Good Samaritan, who helped the wounded Jew lying on the side of the Jericho road. Our neighbour is whoever depends on us for help which it is in our power to give. So we have to live our lives for the good of our neighbours and not just for our own selfish enjoyment.

Christ also preached the two parables of the talents and the pounds, in each case given by a lord to his servants to make use of until he came back. Those who multiplied their talents were commended and the man who buried his talent was condemned in the strongest terms. So God has given each of us talents which we are to multiply and for the use of which we will be accountable at the day of judgment.

The idea that science should be used 'for the relief of man's estate' springs directly from this teaching. Science was not knowledge for its own sake, but must be used to develop medicines and treatments for illness, to relieve poverty and develop the common wealth. It created a generation who not only worked hard and purposefully, but who had, for the first time, an ambition to develop better ways of working.

The result was a sharp increase in wealth. But, unlike the feudal aristocracy, the Puritans saw no need to spend their wealth in ostentation. They did not ape the aristocracy. They lived soberly and used their surplus money to build up capital to develop their businesses. The old merchants' houses which we can still see by the canals of Amsterdam embody this solid and unostentatious spirit.

The French Protestants, the Hugenots, were the heart of the French economy. They had no time for the monopolies and protection of Colbert, the French minister of commerce. When he asked them what he could do for them, their message was to let them get on with it and not to block their trade routes by local taxes and tariffs. They said, '*Laissez faire et laissez passer.*' The economic power of the France of Versailles was built on Hugenot thrift. In 1686 Louis XIV, in his folly, revoked his grandfather's act of protection for the Hugenots, the Edict of Nantes. The Hugenots emigrated to Britain, the Netherlands, Prussia and America – to the great advantage of all four nations – and France went into a long decline, ending in bloody revolution a century later.

The Dutch have a saying, 'God gave us only sea, sand and wind, but he gave us John Calvin and that was enough.' The Swiss match that with the divine gift of 'only snow, rock and ice' – and John Calvin. These two Protestant countries, with very few natural resources, pulled themselves up by their bootstraps to be the most prosperous countries in the world; but never ostentatious with it. The same might be said for Scotland and, indeed, Prussia, whose area at the time was small and whose land was mainly lakes and forests. But in terms of absolute growth, England and America did best of all.

Another vital part of the Protestant ethic was honesty. Seventeenth-century Protestants would not have thought this anything new for a Christian. But the emergence of a whole class of merchants, who commanded the trust of both buyer and seller, was something new. Buyers and sellers could deal freely with people whom they did not know personally and this enabled the flow of trade to be greatly enlarged. It also, in due course, encouraged a much wider public to lend them their money as bankers and to support the great expansion of commerce through London and Amsterdam.

But, by the beginning of the eighteenth century, the first flower of the Protestant ethic was waning. The dynamic impetus of Christian ethics to secular society had died down. The great Puritan leaders had died and, until Wesley and Whitefield arrived, the selfish and cynical dominated the leadership of society. So in Britain, the new wealth created by the Puritans was poured into the old wineskins of the Whig aristocracy. The Puritans had thought through the ethics of work, but had not got round to the ethics of a wealth such as they had never anticipated. The Whig aristocracy – whose plump, satisfied faces under powdered wigs look down on us from the walls of the great houses they built on England's new wealth – were well pleased with the world as it was. The wigs might well have gone to the guillotine with those of the French aristocrats had it not been for a powerful revival of the Christian faith in the mid-eighteenth century – the Methodist movement.

The Methodists

The leaders of this movement were the Wesley brothers – John and Charles – and George Whitefield, all Church of England clergymen, and Selina, Countess of Huntingdon. Its hymn writers were Charles Wesley, Isaac Watts, John Newton and William Cowper. We know far more about their private lives than we do about most of the Reformers and Puritans, and we know that all of them had an experience of conversion which changed their lives profoundly and made them want to share this change with others. But this enthusiasm and insistence on conversion for those already baptised was very disturbing to the established church, who began to bar their pulpits, forcing Wesley and Whitefield to preach in the open air.

To Clapham Common, Bunhill Fields, Kingswood in Bristol, Gwennap Pit in Cornwall, thousands of ordinary people flocked to listen and, over the years, hundreds of thousands were converted and their lives were as profoundly changed as those of their leaders.

The Wesleys and Whitefield never formally left the Church of England. The Countess was entitled to appoint chaplains wherever she went and she set up chapels up and down the country, many of which remain to this day. John Wesley, the organiser of the movement, set up small societies in which rich and poor met together, all contributing what financial support they could, with the rich making up any deficit.

The Puritans had failed to gain control of the national church, but the ethics they had left behind now found a home in the Methodist movement; the care for neighbours, the work ethic, the moderate lifestyle all found their place in the new Methodist church. And a century after John Wesley's death at a good old age, the deacons of the Methodist churches in the great industrial cities were among the founders of the trades union movement, dedicated to the correction of the imbalance of power and wealth between capital and labour.

Even at the end of the eighteenth century, the Methodist movement had begun to have an influence outside its own churches. The Countess of Huntingdon had influenced her own class, asking Whitefield and others to come to speak in her drawing-room, and there was a steady stream of conversions among the aristocracy. At the end of the eighteenth century and the beginning of the nineteenth, there was a group of leading bankers and MPs, known as the Clapham Sect. Its best-known member was William Wilberforce, an MP for Yorkshire and leader of the movement for the abolition, first of the slave trade and then of slavery itself.

The evangelical reformers

The Church of England did not become Methodist, but soon had a group of clergy who also stood in the Puritan tradition. Known as evangelicals, they became the most active and influential group in the church until the arrival of the mid-nineteenth century High Church movement. The wigs and fancy clothing of the eighteenth century gave way to the sober black of the nineteenth, and even the unreformed House of Commons accepted that it had to yield to the pressure for the more representative franchise of the great Reform Act of 1832.

The successor of William Wilberforce as leader of the evangelicals was Lord Ashley, later Earl of Shaftesbury. He was one of the first presidents of the Evangelical Alliance, which brought together evangelicals across all the denominations.

Where Wilberforce had had to concentrate on one major issue, Shaftesbury was able to mobilise the conscience of the early and mid-Victorian church on a wide range of human needs. He started with a successful battle to limit the hours which children should be allowed to work in factories; went on to organise the reform of lunatic asylums; and his best-known work, which packed the streets of London for his funeral, was the 'ragged schools' for the street children of London. He set the pace of mid-Victorian reform, including the work of Florence Nightingale in the hospitals.

As with the Puritans and Methodists, reform and evangelism went together. Shaftesbury said that God had made both body and soul and if God cared for both, so should we. Christian love could not be split into compartments. A hundred years after the Methodists had revived the Christian church, mid-Victorian Britain had its own revival, starting spontaneously in 1859 and reaching every part of the British Isles. Its leading preacher was Charles Haddon Spurgeon whose church was soon unable to hold his congregations. He moved to the Surrey Music Hall, while a great church was built at the Elephant and Castle, seating six thousand and packed to capacity.

In the same year as the revival, Charles Darwin published *The Origin of Species* and by the end of the century – thanks mainly to the immensely able publicity of his friend, Thomas Huxley – the theory of evolution had been accepted as a scientific fact by most of educated society. The churches found themselves forced on the defensive by the general supposition that science had undermined the reliability of the Bible and dispensed with the need for a belief in God.

The churches should and could have stood their ground. Evolution was only a plausible theory; but it presented immense difficulties. Darwin himself admitted that it might seem inconceivable that the human eye – self-regulating for light and focus, self-cleaning, self-protecting by the instant blink and recording everything in detail and in colour – was an accident and not the product of a great designer. But, more important, Darwinism went back on the key principle by which Bacon and the founders of experimental science had separated it from metaphysics; the scientific method is confined to secondary causes. It cannot and, as Bacon said, should not, try to enquire into the primary cause; that is to confuse science with speculation.

Late-Victorian churches take a wrong turning

The problem was that the late-Victorian church had taken a wrong turning. It had started to look inwards, to be more interested in personal spiritual experience than in the needs of its neighbours. Its holiness conventions turned the minds of Christians away from their duty to others and in towards themselves. The liberal wing of the churches, which tagged along with the world's view that science had disproved the final authority of the Bible, stepped smartly into the vacuum with a new gospel: that society would be saved not by redemption through Jesus Christ, but by social action. It fitted well with the enormous optimism of late-Victorian and Edwardian society. Charles Spurgeon fought it in his own Baptist Union, but the majority repudiated him and he withdrew from the union.

Into this vacuum of belief stepped nationalism and jingoistic imperialism. Queen Victoria, against the strong advice of the aged Shaftesbury, became Empress.

The nationalism which led to World War I was supported by the majority of the churches, but the huge slaughter smashed Edwardian optimism and the returning survivors of the Somme and Passchendaele did not return to church. To the new Russian Communist government, Darwin was a hero. They believed in the survival of the fittest economic and political system, and the destruction of all others. The new German dictator, Hitler, and his National Socialists also believed in the survival of the fittest; in their case it was the German race. Where fifteen million Europeans perished in World War I, thirty-five million perished in World War II, the greatest slaughter in human history.

We emerged in 1945, impoverished but thankful. We had had national days of prayer and saw as acts of God the deliverance of our army from Dunkirk and that of our air force which had committed its last reserves to the Battle of Britain's decisive encounter on 15 September 1940.

The post-war settlements

We were pledged, with the other victorious democracies, to a great many 'never agains'. There was the European Declaration of Human Rights, signed in 1947 – wholly Christian in content, though secular in presentation; and there was a Court of Human Rights at Strasbourg to administer it. There was the United Nations, dedicated to resolve conflicts by peaceful means. There was a ringing call by Winston Churchill for a united Europe. There was $75 billion (current values) from the United States in Marshall Aid to reconstruct war-shattered Europe, together with the Organisation for European Economic Cooperation, to help decide who got what and to set conditions for economic cooperation.

The International Monetary Fund was set up to avoid the pre-war competitive currency devaluations and to keep key currencies stable by linking them to the dollar, which was itself tied to gold. The General Agreement on Tariffs and Trade was established to lower the pre-war trade barriers.

When the Soviet Union used its domination of Central Europe to overthrow the democratic Czech government, the North Atlantic Treaty Organisation (NATO) was formed to defend democratic Western Europe. And, following the discovery of the full extent of the Nazi holocaust and the murder of six million Jews, racial discrimination was repudiated and there was no doubt that everyone meant it too.

Above all, the victors did their best to reconstruct a democratic Germany; the democrats in Germany came out of prison to make it work and the old enemies – France and Germany – not only swore that they would never fight again, but began to set up institutions of partnership, out of which, ten years after the war, emerged the Treaty of Messina and then the European Economic Community.

A war-weary Britain decided that, faced with demands for independence, it could no longer afford to police the empire which it had collected along its trade routes 'in a fit of absence of mind'. Starting with India in 1947, the Union Jack was lowered in country after country. The British district officers who had seen fair play, with little but their competence and impartiality to back them, went home for good to a country which, as the American Dean Acheson then said, had 'lost an empire and yet not found a role'.

In the mid-1950s the leadership of Europe had been there for the taking. France and Germany were old enemies with mutual suspicions and if Britain had joined the new EEC at the beginning, we would have been the decisive voice in a troika of the three most powerful countries. Instead we were governed by nostalgia for the temporary empire which had not yet quite disappeared and by the illusion of a special relationship with the United States, despite the stated policy of its government that we would serve old friendships best if we joined the EEC. We applied to join four years too late, were kept out for another twelve and, by the time we arrived in 1973, we had a chip on our shoulder and were forgetful of the fact that leadership goes to those who are committed to the objectives of the joint enterprise and not to its critics.

The country's residual Christian faith did not long survive the war. Liberal churches continued to empty and the evangelicals were still committed to an inward-looking pietism. That did not prevent arm's-length mass evangelism and, as well as home-grown evangelists, Billy Graham came for a first crusade in 1954. But as the churches moved out to the prosperous suburbs, the gulf between the church and the rest of the world widened.

Yet the foundations were being rebuilt. The thirty-year ministry of Martyn Lloyd-Jones at Westminster Chapel in the heart of the capital filled that great building with fifteen hundred on Sunday mornings and two thousand in the evenings. Here was someone who owed nothing to the evangelicals who had followed Spurgeon; a brilliant physician who made no concessions to metaphysics posing as science; a theologian who owed more to the Puritans than to liberal theological colleges; a physician of souls, who could distinguish clinical from spiritual depression; and who, as he started his ministry in South Wales, would willingly spend an evening to diagnose an intractable medical case.

As wartime president, he helped Dr Douglas Johnson build up the Inter-Varsity Fellowship of Evangelical Unions until it is today – as the Universities and Colleges Christian Fellowship – the largest voluntary student body in most universities, from whose graduates come the Christian Medical Fellowship and similar bodies in a dozen professions.

So a church is being rebuilt which can, once more, make a reasoned case for a Christian way of life. Meanwhile, in the sixties, Britain went off in the opposite direction. For the first time for a thousand years, the Christian faith ceased to be the prime moral guide for the law and custom of our country. The permissive legislation of the sixties followed the popular mood; that on moral issues, especially sexual issues, people could do what they thought best and we have already looked at the results of that moral chaos.

But if permissiveness is right for the bedroom, who is to say that it is wrong for the boardroom? Why should directors not use their position to award themselves million-pound bonuses? If passion can prevail over commitment in marriage, why not in our mood towards the minority communities in Britain or our European partners? The question is whether the new and unproven 'political correctness' is enough, or whether we need the strong and proven ethic which has formed our national identity and which alone can preserve it.

Chapter Ten

THE PROTECTION OF FREEDOM

The case for democracy

I was canvassing round old folks' bungalows in the Fens. A door opened and an old man said, 'Isn't democracy wonderful; that you have to come to an old man like me and ask for my vote.' He was right. Democracy is a wonderful thing. In big business and in Whitehall, people are full of their own importance. But an election tests the true measure of your worth. Elections are dedicated to the taking apart of pomposities; to forcing those who want to be elected or re-elected to listen to what ordinary people are actually saying; to tearing apart the fond illusions of those who are in power; to making them spell out just how they are going to fulfil their promises; and to warning them against the folly of ignoring public opinion. It is the time for frank dialogue between rulers and ruled.

If politicians are wise, they do not wait for an election before they listen to what people are saying. Good members of parliament will make sure that they keep in close touch with their constituency. In America, where the House of Representatives has to be re-elected every two years, they keep in very close touch indeed, despite the great distances and as many as half a million electors in each congressional district. The late Speaker Tip O'Neill said, 'Americans like to keep their Congressmen on a tight rein.'

Voters are not always right; but if they know that their MP is listening, then they are willing to listen in return. I spent a morning in the early 1980s with one of my Yorkshire colleagues in the county hall in Wakefield, discussing with county councillors and others what could be done about the soaring rate of unemployment. I came down the A1 in the afternoon to an evening meeting with my own constituents in Cambridgeshire, where the local economy was expanding and prosperous and they saw no need to do anything. We had a spirited dialogue; good for me and, I hope, good for them. My very experienced agent, Andrew Thompson, said that that was what politics was all about.

In the mid-1960s, when I worked for the First Secretary of State, the populist George Brown, he used to tell the assembled Whitehall mandarins, 'But that's not what they say in the pubs in Swadlincote.' So the likely reaction in Swadlincote became a touchstone for what we proposed. Whenever we went with him on visits to factories or mining towns, he was in instant conversation with all around him. They felt he was on their side, and they were right.

Despite the vigour of political dialogue, there are still some politicians who can be pompous and self-opinionated. But when they are out on the stump, there is always someone who brings them sharply down to earth. I well remember one such candidate, wide-eyed, backing out of the local Woolworth's pursued by such a barrage of vulgar, but pointed, abuse as I had seldom heard before. And such pomposity as they do have is nothing to that of those who hold forth without having encountered the occupational hazard of direct encounter with angry citizens.

No system can be perfect, so the success of any system must depend on the speed at which signals of malfunction feed back to those in control. On-line computers give instant feedback and instant correction. Feedback to government is given by the democratic system.

When Mrs Thatcher, from the bunker of No. 10 Downing Street, decided on a poll tax instead of council rates, it was not long before constituency activists from all over the country were reporting to their MPs that the public would not buy it. She did not give in without a struggle, but, in the end, the poll tax went and so did she.

To counter this, autocratic governments have secret police to report back on the morale of the people. But that makes government totally dependent on a source which can easily

164

become corrupted by its own power. Reading *Spycatcher* makes one wonder whether anyone should ever take notice of a trade in lies in which it seems impossible to distinguish between genuine information and plausible counter-information.

But, more important, public accountability now forces government to allow some kind of public debate before even committing itself on new policies. Constitutionally, parliament should have first sight of a new proposal; but the tightly whipped two-party system makes difficult a really helpful constructive exchange of ideas in the Commons. So a debate is launched by unattributable briefing by ministers and is then conducted in the media, giving government an idea of the pros and cons before they commit themselves to a firm proposition to parliament. In this media debate, all kinds of experts can give their views and argue with each other. By the end of it, government should know both whether their idea is feasible and whether the electorate as a whole will support it.

Autocracies have no such safeguard. There is always a smug complacency in the delegations to the European Parliament from countries with autocratic regimes, while in those from democratic countries there is always a sharp sense of political reality. Their feet are on the ground, they know what can be done and what cannot. Autocratic attitudes take time to wear off. Even Boris Yeltsin, newly elected as President of Russia when he came to the European Parliament, clearly had no idea of the economic problems he was about to face. He was surrounded by a coterie of economists, whose untested monetarist proposals he had accepted without any critical feedback. He could have had it from the Russian Parliament, from which a delegation also paid us a visit. He did not find out that he was wrong until that parliament had been abolished and a more amenable one put in its place.

The power of the press

Yet we have always to be sure that we ourselves do not become complacent. Systems, even democratic systems, tend to ossify. New situations arise. All Mr Gladstone's speeches used to be reported verbatim, column after column in the press. Now political reporting is in soundbites to camera on College Green. The editors – rather than the Speaker – decide whose views go to the public. Politicians are shown making speeches, but not heard. The 'words over' come from the TV commentator. And when you knock on your constituents' doors, they quote TV back at you. They clearly believe that if what you tell them has not been on TV it cannot be important, or if it is not the line taken on TV, it cannot be true. So the media are no longer just reporters. What they include and how they report it have become critical factors in most national elections.

In America, politicians try to counter this by buying their own time on TV, so the cost of elections has soared and the need to find vast sums to pay for elections has given enormous power to those who find the funds. I asked a young Congressman how he raised the million dollars he needed for his campaign. He said, 'Business want access and I want cash, so we do a trade.' But that trading process gives the gun lobby a hold on Congress which prevents their listening to the voices of the voters.

In Britain, candidates cannot buy TV time and are strictly limited in their election expenses. The problem has only arisen at a national level, though that is bad enough if the campaign is dominated by the views of the billionaires who control two-thirds of the media. The tabloids are certainly dominated by billionaires, so the maintenance of their monopolies governs the views which are put across with such punch. There are a few national broadsheets which have kept their independence, but the saving grace has been the continued independence of most of the provincial press and that is another reason for returning political power to the provinces.

Christians, who believe in original sin, are more inclined than most to believe that power corrupts and that concentrations of power should be broken up. That would put us against monopoly in broadcasting and the press, in favour of local radio and TV. In America, where there is hardly any national press, the local papers buy in such national comment as they feel they need; so the journalistic expertise is available locally, but what is printed across the nation does not depend on the views of two or three billionaires. In Germany, too, the daily broadsheets are all provincially based and there is only one national daily tabloid – though I used to notice my German colleagues reading it carefully from cover to cover!

Billionaires apart, do journalists have too much unaccountable power? Journalists, when you put this to them, protest that all they are doing is reflecting the views of politicians and people and that, except in articles of opinion, they do not push their own views. And it is certainly true that we are inclined to buy the papers and watch the TV programmes which reflect our own preferences and to turn off the programmes which irritate us. And, in a paper we like, we may well put up with views which we like a lot less. Many people bought the old *Daily Express* for the Maudie Littlehampton cartoon and not for the Empire Free Trade crusader on the masthead; as they bought the *Daily Worker* for its racing tips and not for its Communist propaganda. Robin Day once said that, despite his long years in front of the camera, nothing had come of most of his own political ideals.

Yet that is too simple a view. An editor has to decide which items to print and which to spike. For five years, in the days in which its discussions ranked as a major news item, I took the press conference after the monthly meeting of the National Economic Development Council. There was then one eminent national broadsheet which printed the news which accorded with its owner's views and simply omitted all the news which did not.

The other problem is, as I found when I was trying to correct the story related in Chapter 4 about my company's highland smelters, that journalists tend to hunt in packs. They pick up stories from each other and they do not feel comfortable in taking a line which is quite opposite to that taken by all the other papers, since that would make their editor worry. So they all tend to take up the same subject and run with it and to ignore other issues. Although they do not take a similar line on critical issues, they tend to share the same broad assumptions.

For long the media would not report the debates in the European Parliament, so when all the critical issues which had been addressed in Europe finally made an impact at home, they came as a great shock. But by then the political debate in Europe was over and it was too late for anyone at Westminster to do anything about them.

So, for good or ill, there is a 'power of the press'; and since power corrupts and can be abused we should see that, so far as possible, it is diffused; that oligopolies are curtailed; that outlets are multiplied and that a few powerful people are not allowed to decide what it is that we see and hear.

The diffusion of political power

Diffusion of power in the media is only the beginning. The British constitution has allowed far too much concentration of power in the hands of national government. Our constitution stems from the agreement among the English upper classes over three hundred years ago to take power from the monarchy and give it to a parliament controlled by the great landed families. For the next hundred and fifty years, the Whigs and Tories kept control. It was not what we today would call a democracy. They passed Acts of Parliament enclosing the common land and they moved out of the homely village manors and set up great Italianate palaces, standing alone and remote in the middle of broad parklands. The ordinary people had no part in this and the Whigs and Tories were, as we have seen, probably saved from revolution only by the Methodist revival among the working classes.

The Reform Acts of 1832 and 1867 were concessions wrung from a reluctant oligarchy, but the basic framework of the constitution remained the same. The Whig and Tory oligarchies were more interested in retaining the power of the state for their alternate use than in creating a constitution which gave the citizen enduring safeguards against government. The veto of the House of Lords was only curtailed in 1910 and the old parties kept their grip on power until 1945. Even in the 1980s, the *Yes, Minister* TV series reflected accurately the relationship between the unelected Establishment – as represented by Sir Humphrey – and the minister nominally and temporarily in power, but no match for the smooth organisation of that Establishment.

By contrast, almost all other democracies were formed from scratch, and the primary object of their constitutions was the diffusion of power and the accountability of state power in particular. All their constitutions were written documents, which set out the conditions under which power could be exercised. We, alone, do not have a written constitution. Its absence is said to give more flexibility to meet new conditions as they arrive. But it can only give flexibility to the insider, to those for whom the absence of written law makes it much easier to find and twist precedents and to do whatever government finds convenient.

What happens when there is an enquiry, which shows that government has broken its own guidelines for the export of military equipment? Ministers say that they did not know what was happening in their departments and civil servants say that they were obeying orders. No one resigns and no one is dismissed. Yet, but for a chance enquiry, the exporters who had been assured informally that the sale was in order would have gone to prison. Ministers who are clearly responsible for what has gone wrong are no longer inclined to resign and no one obliges them to go. Every time there is no action, it is a precedent for future inaction.

A determined government can easily enlarge its power by testing the limits of our flexible constitution. The civil service is meant to be independent of the government but there is no constitutional machinery to see that this status is respected by government. Two very senior permanent secretaries who were found to be too independent were not elevated to the Lords as all their predecessors had been. That gave the strongest possible signal for the career prospects of all who were coming on. The head of the civil service was sent off to protect the government in the Australian courts and was subject to public mockery – another signal of total dependence of the civil service on the government in office. At a lower level, appointments reflected the answer to the question, 'Is he/she one of us?'

It used to be argued that the monarch had residual powers. After all, everything government does is done in the name of the monarch. That was one good reason for making the monarch financially independent. But once a monarch is made to pay taxes like everyone else, they are beholden to the government which raises the taxes. Once a government can insist that a public hall – in a castle in which the monarch has private apartments – has to be repaired at the monarch's own expense, the monarch can hardly have enough residual power to summon a prime minister for overstepping the mark.

What has happened in our unwritten constitution is that the power of the Crown has been taken over in toto by the government of the day without any Acts of Parliament specifying the extent and limits of that power. Orders in Council, which is the monarch's Council, are promulgated without parliamentary approval, so MPs find it hard to keep up with what is being done in the name of the Crown. The unwritten constitution is a delegation from the top down and does not, as with all written constitutions, spring upwards from the people as a temporary authority given to government under strict conditions and for which they are strictly accountable to the people's elected representatives.

A written constitution – the head of state

All written constitutions have a head of state and either the head of state or the Speaker of the parliament has the task of dealing with changes of government. So a British constitution should give explicit power and authority to the head of state – in our case the monarch – and have explicit rules for the replacement of a head of state. If the head of state is to be a monarch, then the constitution should incorporate the precedent that parliament can, if need be, select from the royal house the person most suitable for the post. The new monarch need not be in the direct line – George I was not – and can even be the husband of someone in the royal house – as was William III. For a head of state, there is an important job of representing the nation abroad and, to put it in the words of the apostle Paul to the Romans, 'to encourage the good' in the nation by public recognition of those who have given most to the community. Above all, the head of state should give encouragement by personal example. It is a job which requires the ability to command universal respect; the ability to suffer fools gladly; to forgo personal opinions, especially on politics, which would alienate large groups of people; and qualities of tact, diplomacy and great personal patience.

It also requires one other very important quality: the courage, probably at short notice, to stand up to a potential dictator. King Constantine of Greece failed in this test, but King Juan Carlos of Spain saved Spanish democracy by swift personal intervention, when he went on radio late at night to condemn a military coup and command the obedience of the army. Juan Carlos has maybe the most vital characteristic of a head of state in such a crisis: a dignity which commands instant respect. Nelson Mandela has this innate dignity, as did President Wiesacker of Germany and so does our present Queen Elizabeth.

The head of state – or the Speaker – is the personification of the written constitution. So the present unwritten powers of the monarch need to be made into quite explicit powers and enlarged to enable a British head of state to protect the constitution. If it is thought not possible to give enlarged powers to a monarch who has no popular mandate, then it should be possible for the House of Commons – by weighted majority – to choose a head of state, who could well be the monarch.

The protection of the constitution should not be left to the head of state alone, but should be the duty of a constitutional court. Since at present parliament is sovereign, it sits in judgment on itself and, in practice, the government majority ensures that no action is taken which can harm the government. Or the government sets up commissions of enquiry and then takes no notice of their recommendations. A constitutional court makes sure that our rulers are not judge and jury on their own conduct. We should, for the protection of the citizen, embody the European Declaration of Human Rights (which predates the European Economic Community by ten years) in British law.

Government by the majority

Democracy is defined as government by the majority, with the consent of the minority. In Britain it is, by contrast, government by the minority with the consent of the majority. That is the overwhelming reason for constitutional change. Our present quaint system elects the candidate with the largest number of votes, even though they may not have an overall majority. That has made it impossible in almost any British election for government to command the support of the majority of the electors, which hardly helps to gain their consent for all that government does in their name in the next five years. The present system would be especially dangerous if it allowed a large authoritarian party to undermine the legitimacy of an elected government and disastrous if, as a result, that government were unable to maintain public order.

But it is above all unfair. Its justification is that it usually produces a clear winner, who can get on and govern without the need to form a coalition, because, 'The Queen's government must be carried on.' But that is an argument for the convenience of government, not a democratic argument. For it unfailingly produces governments for which the majority of the electors have not voted. Coalitions are a democratic device for making sure that a government takes into account the views of the majority of the electors. They temper down narrow 'conviction politics' in a government which will carry a broader base of agreement.

Government based on a majority of the voters also makes for wider choice. Instead of two major parties, each composed of uneasy internal coalitions, it enables the voters to decide for themselves what shade of party opinion best represents their views. If government had to represent a majority of voters, the British government would not have been paralysed for several years past by an unworkable coalition between unionists and nationalists. The nationalists would have formed their own party and would have found out how many voters supported them. Judging by the German and French experience in national elections, they might have got between 7 per cent and 15 per cent of the votes. The Liberals and Social Democrats would not have had to merge and might have had a larger vote if there were not the argument that a vote for them would be wasted. A vote for the Greens, too, need not be a wasted vote.

The business of coalition-forming would then be out in the open and would be healthier and less hypocritical. The two big parties would no longer have to fudge their election manifestos behind closed doors. Each party would stand on a platform nearer to its supporters' aims and, if it wanted to be in government, it would then have to decide what it was prepared to give up in return for the power to carry out those of its policies which its coalition partners would agree to support.

Extremists on the fringes would no longer have the power to hold the major parties to ransom. Power would come from the centre and not from the extremes. In the seventies, the Labour Party was prey to the extreme left and more lately the Conservative Party has been prey to the nationalist right. So the present system tends to produce extreme swings of policy, when each government undoes what its predecessor has done and there is a disruptive discontinuity in national policy. Centre-right and centre-left coalitions give the political stability from which continental Europe has benefited so much.

A most important benefit would be the return of political power and respect to the House of Commons. In coalition politics, the views of the individual MP matter more, as does the parliamentary argument. It is clear, both from the attendance today in the chamber and in the style of debate, that the Commons is no longer where the decisions are made. The government usually commands an overall majority for its full term and its supporters are in the chamber to cheer it on and its opponents are there to jeer. Neither represents an edifying spectacle to the public and does great disservice to the ideal of democracy.

In the multiparty European Parliament, where I was a member for fifteen years, neither of the two big parties – Social Democrats and Christian Democrats – had a majority. So members were courteous in debate to colleagues from other parties, because at some point they might want their votes. While, of course, party points were made in debates, there was (and still is) a real effort to convince members of other parties of the validity of the case being put; an effort which is even more marked in the committees where a lot of the decisions are taken.

This also has the effect of making the administration – the European Commission – much more open, because if their proposals are to go through they cannot hide behind one party, they must be available to all parties. When Commissioners come to full sessions, they have to be really persuasive and to come back with alternatives if what they propose is not acceptable.

It might be argued that this is to give altogether too much power to elected politicians; that being elected does not make up for the expertise of the civil servant. But that is to misunderstand the difference between the two functions. The elected politician is there to reflect the needs and will of the public. They have in mind the people whom they meet every weekend – all their hopes and fears, all their needs and ambitions – and they are there, first of all, to give a general sense of priorities and of political direction, which the civil servant needs. So they must also examine rigorously the proposals which the civil servant makes, to make sure that they meet the situation.

I have two vividly contrasting experiences: the Single European Act, which sprang from the European Parliament and went through the whole democratic process; and the Maastricht Treaty, produced by experts from behind closed doors.

The Single European Act, which removed the final barriers to trade between the member states, started with the six chairman of the parliament's economic and trade committees, who were worried about the rising rate of unemployment in the early 1980s. We commissioned two economists – Michel Albert and James Ball – who produced a report, widely reported in the continental media, which was then examined by a special committee of the parliament, which held public hearings. The European Parliament debated its committee's report and voted for proposals for the complete abolition of trade barriers between member states. These proposals were in the 1984 election manifestos of the major parties and we returned after the election with public support. We explained it in November to the Council of Ministers; early the next year the new Commission made it the central part of their programme; and the final proposals for the Single European Act were approved by both Council and Parliament and ratified without difficulty by all twelve national parliaments.

By contrast, the Maastricht Treaty proposals started with a remit from behind the closed doors of the Council of Ministers to the twelve central bank governors, who met behind even more firmly closed doors. They were asked how, if there were to be monetary union, it could be carried out. This was an important technical question, asked of most competent technical experts; but it also had enormous political repercussions, which could not be answered by central bank governors. But they were not referred to the European Parliament, which had been working on the problem and had some helpful answers.

The political questions were,

- to whom would a new European central bank be accountable?

- what would be the effect of a single currency on poorer regions?
- what would be the effect on economic growth?
- would there be any countervailing power at European level to promote economic growth with the same dedication as the central bank promoted a sound currency?
- to what extent, if at all, would this need fiscal powers at European level?
- could the central bank contain inflation as firmly as the Bundesbank? (especially important for the Germans)
- what would be the advantages to Europe of a single currency in our trade and monetary policy in the rest of the world, especially with Japan and the United States?

That is a formidable list of questions and none of them were answered. Indeed they are only now, seven years later, becoming part of the debate in Britain. Instead of answering them, the twelve heads of government, not all following the technical details, sat well into the night and then signed the treaty on behalf of their governments.

The result of asking technical experts to take the lead rather than putting it to an open parliamentary process was political chaos. The Danish government had not consulted its own special Folketing Committee and, with added ineptitude, circulated the Maastricht Treaty without explanation to all post offices. Since the treaty was a proposed amendment to the Treaty of Rome, as amended by the Single European Act, no one except a constitutional lawyer could be expected to understand the document in the Danish post offices. By a narrow majority, the very democratic Danish electorate voted against it. Only extremely skilled chairmanship by John Major at the next European Council was able to obtain amendments which allowed the question to be put to the Danish people again to get a majority in favour.

The French also had a referendum, which was only won by a slim majority. The first Danish referendum result alerted the House of Commons, which gave the British government a long hot summer, as the treaty had to go through line by line against a combination of right-wing nationalists – quite prepared to bring down their own government – and a Labour opposition intent on defeating the government, even though they supported the proposals.

There are no short cuts. Changes should be based on the need for public understanding and consent.

Safer and fairer electoral systems

The debate on the reform of voting systems is based on rather boring arguments on the exact method and, because they are technical, they do not get public support. Whichever method is chosen is safer and fairer than government based on a minority of voters.

The French have two-tier elections and the American system of primaries gives a similar result. In France all parties vote in the first election. The second is a run-off between those with the highest votes preceded by negotiations in which the smaller parties bargain with the larger, who have to take their views into account before gaining their support for the run-off.

The Irish have a single transferable vote in multi-member constituencies. The second preference votes of those members with least votes are added to the rest until, by process of elimination, five (or whatever the number of members for the constituency) emerge as the winners. This enables the larger of the smaller parties to win seats. The same system is used in Northern Ireland for the European elections, which makes sure that the 40 per cent Nationalist community is represented.

In the Irish Republic it is still possible for a government party to have an overall majority, but it usually needs one additional party to form a government. The method is not quite so comfortable for the members. As an Irish member once told me, 'Your problem in your constituency is not your opponents, but your colleagues. If one of my colleagues makes a speech in Kells, I have to go to Kells and remind the good folk of that town that I am there too. So we spend all our lives chasing each other round the constituency. We'd far prefer your British system, where none of your colleagues can make a speech in your constituency without your permission; but the good people of Ireland will not let us have it.'

The people of Ireland have good reason. Their system keeps

their members on their toes. It also means that constituents can go to a member of their own party on a problem and do not have to depend on their one sitting member who may not be so sympathetic. Above all, it is fairer. This is the system preferred by most organisations who are lobbying for a change.

Other ways of making government more accountable

Lord Hailsham talked of 'the dictatorship of the majority', which gives absolute power to the government in office until the end of its term. Other countries have ways of curbing this dictatorship, none of which are available to the British citizen.

Most countries have a more or less firm separation between government and the people's representatives. This is most marked in the United States, where there is an absolute separation of the Administration from the Congress. It is not possible to be a Congressman or a Senator and a member of the Administration. Senator Dole had to give up his Senate seat before he ran for the office of president. It is considered to be a full-time job to represent your state or your congressional district and honour enough in itself.

The President of the United States is directly elected and he chooses his cabinet from people of ability and standing, but few have been in Congress. This separation gives the Congress of the United States far more independence and power than the House of Commons. Other countries have similar restrictions. In the Netherlands it is necessary to give up your parliamentary seat to serve in the Dutch government.

In Britain, by contrast, a third of the MPs of the majority party are members of the government and a third of the opposition want to be in government after the next election. But the power of appointment rests with the prime minister and it is made clear by the whips that promotion to office depends on their loyalty. So, in a conflict of interests, they are under strong pressure to put the party before their constituents.

The prospect of becoming a parliamentary secretary may seem no big deal. But parliament, as it is at present, seems to attract those who have little outside qualification and are dependent on achieving office. And the larger the proportion who follow the party line regardless, the less attractive office has become to people with outside reputations and professions who are not dependent on parliament, and the fewer their number among MPs. That makes a case on its own for a stronger role for parliament in its relation to government.

A second chamber

Most countries have a second chamber of parliament, elected on a different basis, often representing the country's regions. In Germany the Bundesrat, which represents the Länder (regions), has a powerful constitutional position and anything of importance needs its agreement. In the United States the Senate also represents the states and has considerable powers, especially on foreign policy. But in Britain an unelected House of Lords cannot be an effective counter to the elected House of Commons. So there is a strong case for a democratic second chamber with enough powers to curb the 'elected dictatorship' based on the Commons. There is also a case for its more mundane task as a revising chamber, so long as it is based directly or indirectly on election. There is no case at all for the present House of Lords with a built-in majority of hereditary peers.

The present House of Lords does contain great expertise, especially on the cross benches, as anyone who has faced the cross-examination of a House of Lords expert committee will testify. The problem is that, because of its lack of a democratic base, its excellent reports gather dust on the library shelves, because government is under no pressure to do anything about them.

Regional government

Since power corrupts, it is a good constitutional principle to spread it widely. It should not be so heavily concentrated in London but we should spread it, as other countries do, between national and regional government. So the weakening of local government in the last two decades has been a move in the wrong direction. It is nearer to the voter than national government, and national parties are built on a stiff framework of local government counsellors.

Before the changes in local government in the early 1970s, I advocated regional government and was opposed by the formidable Dame Evelyn Sharpe, Permanent Secretary of the Ministry of Housing and Local Government, on the grounds that it would be strong enough to weaken the power of central government. She won her battle, as she won most Whitehall battles, and the government went instead for an intermediate layer of larger counties, which were neither near enough to the people and to the old counties and cities to claim local loyalty, nor large enough for activities like roads and health, which are much better done on a regional basis. In my own enlarged county of Cambridgeshire people identify with Peterborough or Cambridge, but, as one Lord Lieutenant said of the two cities, 'Never the twain shall meet'.

But all of the county would identify with East Anglia as would people elsewhere with the West Country, the West Midlands, Yorkshire, Lancashire – each centred on an acknowledged capital city. London most certainly has its loyalties and the Home Counties are unique. And, if there were English regions, it would be no special deal if Scotland and Wales had regional governments too. As it is, the regional functions are carried out by unelected quangos, whose political appointments are part of central government's considerable political patronage.

With regional government, the political life – which has drained away from cities like Edinburgh and Manchester to Westminster – would return to its source among the people of the region. I asked the Lord Mayor of Manchester what he thought and he was strongly in favour! Regional newspapers would matter more than the national ones. People of experience would think it worthwhile to run for election and would take over the reins and responsibility. People are proud of their region and would accept from its government what they would not accept from the distant national capital. After all, Britain has ten times the population it had in the reign of the first Elizabeth and it is time we adjusted to our new size.

Last but not least, looking at the worst-case scenario – which is the job of a constitution – this change would make it much more difficult for an autocratic party if it got enough Commons seats to be within reach of power.

Chapter Eleven

HOLDING SOCIETY TOGETHER

The invisible neighbour

In between the family and the government, there are other institutions which help to hold society together; which help us to get on with and behave better towards one another and which have their own sanctions against those who behave badly.

A great many of these are clubs in which the members share a special interest – cycling, fishing, darts, cricket or, more recently, the gymnasium – but the special interest often confines the club to one age, sex or income group and rarely crosses the lines of social conflict. So far as they make us more sociable and less lonely and isolated, they are all to the good, but they would all be better if they were part of a broader community.

A major problem of late twentieth-century life has been the disappearance of the community. The high-rise blocks of flats destroyed the social network of the back streets, where everyone knew everyone else. If anyone had a problem, there was someone who could help; the children played in the streets and if one of them misbehaved, everyone knew who to complain to. Then they were all put into high-rise flats, no one knew their neighbour, and the communal playground within sight and reach of all the mums disappeared. The walkways became dangerous and at night everyone lived behind locked doors. Alternatively the young wives suffered from 'new town blues'. As the song of the time went, 'They all lived in little boxes, and they all looked just the same.'

Town-planning was for planners and not for people. Cities were zoned, so that everyone had to travel a long way from home to work and back again. There was no spill-over of the communal life in the big factory to the communal life outside it. Everyone lived their own lives and they did not connect naturally to those round about them.

There were still, of course, the shops. But the supermarket was on the way. I was secretary of a multiple grocery company when we introduced the first self-service shop in Coatsworth Road, Gateshead. It was more efficient and customers did not have to wait for service; but for a lot of them, the wait and the chat were part of what they went for and they didn't like it at all. Now the supermarkets have drained the trade away from the local shops and these local social centres are closing down. Suburbs and villages are just places to go home to at night. Even the pubs are thinning out.

In the mid-twentieth century, the cinema was a social centre of sorts; but now TV has closed down half the cinemas, especially those outside the main towns. TV and videos have taken over and when the young want to go out, there is nowhere to go. The buses do not run late and even if they could afford a car, they do not have a licence to drive. The drug-pushers at the school gates offer their wares as a means of 'recreation'.

A popular theme in early twentieth-century novels was the frustration of the young with suburban and provincial life and the urge to get away from their constricting bonds to the excitement of the big city. Now the constricting bonds have been cut to ribbons and a cosy glow of nostalgia rests on the image of the community which we have lost.

So the mood now is to discourage out-of-town shopping, to keep cars out of town centres, to make the shopping streets attractive, filling them with cafes and to make the town the community centre which it once was, with buildings once more built to human scale. All that is a help, but it is nothing like enough to rebuild a sense of community.

The old county of Cambridgeshire has found one answer. Most of our secondary schools are built as community colleges; places which, after school hours, are centres of social activity. The school does not have to organise the activity, but it is available for anyone who does, so that, most nights, the school is a centre of communal activity of one kind or another; people are no longer strangers over a fence; newcomers can take their place much more quickly in the web of friends and neighbours.

The professions

But local loyalties do not make a nation. That needs organisations which are nationwide. I have always thought that the organisations which most clearly follow the Christian ethic are the professions, like doctors, teachers, nurses, engineers, lawyers and vets. I have always believed that the unprecedented burst of prosperity in the last three centuries owes far more to them than it does to capitalism, which is nothing new. It has, after all, been with us throughout recorded history. Job and Abraham both had great wealth, which had a propensity to grow of its own momentum. The professions are quite different.

The professions certainly fulfil Christ's command that we are to multiply our talents. The coming generation is taught the current state of knowledge in a tough learning programme, which may last as long as five years after university or, with medicine, even longer. Teaching is not just left to academics. Practising members of the professions take students on to work with them. Once trained, its members do their best, over their working life, to expand the base of knowledge and improve the practice, and leave both knowledge and practice in a better state than they found it.

They also, at their best, fulfil the Christian principle of service to the community. The first aim of the profession is not to maximise its profits, but to serve. This may be blurred in our very materialistic society in which we are all encouraged to grab what we can. But most teachers are prepared to stay in the profession with their relatively low pay rather than use their skill commercially, as many of them could. Doctors and nurses are prepared to work in a national health service; and move over to a more capitalistic form only when government presses them to do so. And in many industries, the real wealth creators would sooner work at their profession than give it up for the bonuses of the boardroom.

The industrial democracies are knowledge-based societies. Our wealth is not based on our raw materials, since the countries with the least are often the most successful; it is based on putting raw materials to use 'for the relief of man's estate'. The greater our knowledge, the better the use we make of raw materials and the more able we are to replace what we do use. The continuous development of useful knowledge through our learned professions is the key to our economic development. And the dynamic of the profession is not profit but service. Every professional has a duty of care for those they serve.

Of course those at the top of their profession can earn high fees. But, at least until now, they have not been tempted to make more money by cutting corners. They depend on their professional reputation which they cannot put at risk. If they were found to be cutting corners, they would be subject to professional discipline and their earning power would vanish. Those members of a profession who work for a corporation face the same discipline. At one time in my life I knew that if I had to sacrifice my job or my profession quite apart from the rights and wrongs of the particular issue, it would be the job that would have to go.

In today's permissive and materialistic society, professions have to make sure that the duty of care is not undermined. That is at the heart of the euthanasia debate. The duty of the doctor is to preserve the health and life of the patient; so doctors should not be called upon to terminate lives. Old people can so easily be seen by their families as a nuisance to live with or an expense to keep in a home; and maybe the money in the will is badly needed. How would a doctor be able to judge the pressure which made an old lady put her signature on a document asking for her life to be ended? His duty is to her and not to the relatives.

That is not the only ethical issue now facing the medical profession. The great increase in knowledge has enabled doctors to cure illnesses which were previously incurable – but at a price. The great increase in the cost of the health service is a reflection of what can now be done to help the human condition. But, when funding is short, there have to be priorities and often doctors are forced to decide. In the long run it is governments who should decide whether it is to be one rule for the rich and another for the poor, or whether it is still to be a health service for all.

There is also the growing nightmare of Aldous Huxley's *Brave New World*, when eugenics decides which embryo is fertilised and which is not. Already there are pregnant women who are being asked whether, because there is a percentage risk (maybe not all that high) of a malformed or malfunctioning baby, they want an abortion. The medical profession may have to decide whether it is governed by utilitarianism or by ethics.

It is not only in medicine that professions are under pressure. Maybe they did once look to the outsider like a cosy cartel. Certainly there is more pressure on them today to compete. But there was a reason for fixed fees. It was that, unlike a customer buying a bar of soap, the professional clients find it hard to judge the quality and amount of complex work needed for the service for which they are paying.

Savers, on whose money the capital markets depend, put money into banks or pension funds run by people they have never met. The banks and funds lend or invest in companies whose directors they do not know either. They risk their money on the assurance from auditors that the accounts show a true and fair view of the company's trading and assets. If there were any doubt about the integrity of the auditor's certificate, the whole pack of cards would come tumbling down in a stock-market crash.

We rely on the medical profession to stand up against the powerful lobby of the drug companies; on the scientific professions to stand up against the lobby of the food and farming industry when the safety of the food we eat seems to be at risk; on the architects and engineers for the safety standards of our buildings and bridges. In our materialistic society these professions are all under pressure of one kind or another. They do not have the visibility of the politicians or the pressure groups, but they are absolutely essential to our interdependent, knowledge-based society; a set of intermediate institutions which we need to protect because they protect us.

The professions have suffered from the ideology of market forces. If everything is to be decided by supply and demand with as little interference as possible, then there is less room for those who want to insist that standards of conduct matter more. That is all the more reason for making sure professions insist on their codes of ethics and ensure that their members keep

185

to them; all the more reason to worry about the corrosive effect of greed throughout our society.

The trades unions

The trades unions too, despite their bad press, are a cohesive force in society. I worked closely with them when I was in public service between 1964 and 1979 and got to know their leaders well. The ideal of the trades union movement is to use the bargaining power of the strong to help the weak. It is not their fault that their main weapon is negative: the withdrawal of their labour. They are usually most reluctant to use it, because strikes are costly to those who call them. And leaders know that once they get workers out, it can be much more difficult to convince them that the settlement is worthwhile and to get them to go back again. For those reasons, there is a strong tradition in the trades union movement of worker solidarity – that though the minority may not like a decision, they must go with the majority.

To go into the office of the leader of a major union is to enter the history of the working man (they were mostly men). There are the historic banners and shields – all the memories of the struggle when the bosses were strong and the unions were weak and they had to stand shoulder to shoulder.

A very different kind of problem arose from the late sixties, when a gulf opened between the unions like distribution and catering – which were still weak – and those like the electricians, general workers, printers and engineers – which were strong. Members of strong unions worked in big manufacturing plants and in newspaper printing with very expensive plant, where any stoppage cost ten to fifty times as much as a settlement. Unofficial strikes of those who could do most damage pushed up the general wage level for the unions concerned, and this was then followed by all the rest in a frightened scramble. I remember Alf Allen, the distribution trades leader, telling me that during those scrambles their telephones were blocked by incoming calls.

The trades union leaders were well aware that the resulting inflation did their members no good at all and were anxious to do what they could to prevent or slow down the rate of inflation.

There were three attempts to have a concerted wages policy made by the first and second Wilson governments, the Heath government and the Callaghan government. The trades unions, who knew that they had the unprecedented problem of holding unofficial strikes in check, nevertheless gave their cooperation.

The Wilson policy, against the TUC's warning, went on too long. The Heath policy, also against the TUC's advice, was too rigid and broke on the second miners' strike, since the miners had a genuine case. The Callaghan policy also ran on a year too long and the 1978–9 'winter of discontent' was the end of incomes policies. It was also the end of the policy of full employment, which was a major objective of incomes policies. But the failure also did undeserved harm to the reputation of trades unions, who do have a major role as institutions of social cohesion.

Everyone remembers the messy end of the incomes policies, but the figures show that the cooperation of the unions with the Wilson and Callaghan governments produced an optimum combination of high employment, low inflation and an improvement in the trading balance, none of which have been matched since then.

The trades union movement cannot do everything. It could not control the 'flying pickets', which I encountered when I was working with John Laing in the early seventies; nor could it stop 'rent-a-mob' political activists trying to picket sites where they were not recognised by the union whose workers wanted to come to work. Nor did it have control over the miners' leader, Arthur Scargill, when he called a strike without a ballot in the heat of summer when the coal stocks were at their highest. He lost the strike and his own reputation, but he also damaged the reputation of the trades unions.

Company managements have, by now, taken steps to make sure that they are never so vulnerable again. Production and newspaper printing lines are automated; work is subcontracted and double-sourced; fewer people are employed on a permanent basis and, above all, the bargain of full employment has been broken and the rate of unemployment is four to six times what it was in the sixties. With a membership of seven million, the trades unions still matter, but this is a long way below their peak of eleven million.

John Monks, the present TUC General Secretary, seems to be

just the right man for his time. He is thoughtful, intelligent and articulate and should be capable of finding the right role for the movement if the pendulum of political opinion falls back to the centre. He has already begun to look at ways back to full employment and he does not have to win an election, so he can concentrate on the realities of life and does not have to worry about party-political counter-attacks. If we are to have full employment again, management will need to bring the trades unions back into more active partnership and, if they do this, it is as well that government should have an active dialogue with them too.

We should never forget the origins of the trades union movement in Britain. It was the answer of the working people to the new phenomenon of raw capitalism. There was only so much that the statesmen like Lord Shaftesbury could do. In most situations, if working people did not find out how to defend themselves, they would be trampled on. The first trades union leaders were, on Sunday, likely to be deacons in the local Methodist chapel and they brought to their union job all their Christian belief in the dignity of working people and the dignity of labour as a calling of God. To the trades unionist as to the democratic politician it is, in the end, people who matter. And people need protection today just as much as they did when the trades unions were founded.

The corporation

In trying to see how to keep society together, we need to ask whether the company is just a place in which we work for a living, as the supermarket is just a place in which we shop. I do not believe that there is any future in paternalism outside the small private company. But nor do I believe that a thousand people working together are just a collection of random economic inputs. In all my experience, companies cannot work well without good human relationships, and the formation of constructive human relationships should be of interest to the Christian.

There is an increasing gulf between those who own companies and those who work in them. Originally the boss had a face and a character which was known to those who worked in his (seldom her) business. When the public company first developed, the chairman and managing director might no longer have voting control, but they were at the helm, just as they had been before. Praise or blame, they were responsible. Now, with the hostile takeover bid, no one knows who their boss is going to be tomorrow. So there is an even stronger reason today to create a partnership between those working in a company.

Britain has been torn between the American and the North European styles of management. Although, at the time of writing, American unemployment is lower than ours and unemployment in the core of the European Union is higher, there are strong arguments for going the European way. If our European partners achieve higher employment at which they aim, they already have a partnership with their unions which will help them to continue to restrain inflation. We do not have this partnership, nor do the Americans.

Walking round shop floors I have found that there is a huge contrast between those managements who work closely with employees and those who do not. I was involved in the 'Export Year' 1976–7, when there were over a thousand 'Export Year Committees' where management and shop floor together worked out ways of improving the company's service to its export markets. We had many examples of very positive shop-floor contributions and – no doubt for other reasons too – the country's volume of exports went up by 10 per cent.

Stakeholding is not just a slogan, there is a moral case as well as a practical case for partnership. Small companies may not need it, since relations are likely to be close in any case. But large companies are impersonal and difficult to operate in conditions of full employment without an intelligent attempt to build up relations of mutual trust. That needs an ordered dialogue with access to information which enables the employees to make a constructive contribution to the company's decision-making.

The need for an industry/government forum

Until a few years ago industry had a forum for constructive dialogue with government on the industry committees of the NEDC, which

I described in Chapter 6. There is also a political case for it, as a forum which helps to hold together management, unions and government, often at odds with each other. NEDC was continued by the incoming Labour government, despite its new Department of Economic Affairs, and remained a major forum through the Heath and Callaghan governments, being downgraded during the Thatcher government and only wound up in the Major government to settle a cabinet dispute between two senior ministers on which one of them should be in the chair.

That it survived so long in the bleak political climate of monetarism was due to the usefulness of the forum as a meeting place for government, management and the trades unions. Those who actually operate in the open market are much more sceptical about the ability of the market to give the right answer to everything. They know that the market is not perfect. So, just as we need intermediate levels between government and the private citizen, we need intermediate levels between government and industry. Government may talk of market forces, but it is itself one of the forces, controlling about 40 per cent of the national product and, from industry's point of view, it is a clumsy giant.

Not only that, but policies which seem to make sense politically are often disaster to industry and commerce – the policy of low tax and high interest rates among them; or the paralysis on European Monetary Union, because of the pressures of nationalism. Government is always at the receiving end of a powerful political drive from its activists. If industry and commerce, on which our economic future depends, do not have similar access and the publicity which goes with the resultant debate, then policy will be driven by pure ideology. Today the drive for lower taxes is not curbed as it should be from the informed arguments of those who have to deliver the country's economic performance, on which the political aims depend. So, too, a continued high rate of unemployment discourages training, which, like any other investment of time, money and personal energy, depends on there being a market for the finished product.

All these issues need the forum which the NEDC provided and should and could provide again. The monthly meeting of those responsible for the economic health of this trading nation focused its attention on the issues which mattered, and that in turn put pressure for the changes which were needed. Political fantasy was harder to maintain against the realities of making a living in a hard competitive world. It is this challenge to political fantasy which is now lacking in the public debate on our future. The return of NEDC, or something like it, could have a strong cohesive effect. In this and other joint efforts between industry and government – such as the promotion of exports – there was a real feeling of being in it together.

Does the church have a social function?

In the divine economy, there seem to be three basic social organisations: the family, the church and the state. Christians cannot doubt that all three were founded by God and the different functions of each are made clear. In their different ways, all were intended to hold society together, to promote good and to curb evil.

In the thousand years between Constantine and the Reformation, the church was an integral part of society. The local church was the centre of village life. In the towns it was hardly less important. All the efforts of Luther and Calvin were aimed to correct doctrine and practice in the churches, because they were a vital part of the life of the community. It did not occur to them that the church should not be the centre of life in Geneva, Strasbourg or Saxony. In England and Scotland too, the church remained at the centre of life during the sixteenth century. Hard things were said about those like the Anabaptists, who saw the church as a group of believers in the middle of an unbelieving world.

Baptism was the natural dividing line between those who believed that every child in the village should be baptised into the church and those who insisted that baptism was only valid as a recognition of personal faith. The national churches of Scotland, England, Switzerland, the Netherlands, Scandinavia and North Germany all believed in baptism of infants, who were therefore part of the church and this meant that there was no division between the church and society. The church – Catholic, Lutheran, Calvinist, Anglican and later Methodist – was part of society. Only the

Anabaptists, with adult baptism and the doctrine of a 'gathered church', were outside.

I do not raise the issue to rekindle old arguments or emphasise current divisions. But all of us come to the question, 'Is the church part of society?' with certain assumptions. It is helpful if we realise what these are, even if the secular society in which we find ourselves today is much more like that surrounding the early church or in the dark ages than life in a 'Christian society'.

As I go round the country looking at the social work of the churches, there is a strong remnant in the state churches of the feeling that, though society is secular, the whole parish is still the responsibility of the church and that, at national level, whether Scotland or England, the national church still has a duty to the nation and its leaders a duty to give a moral lead.

At the other extreme of church order, the new community churches also feel a strong sense of responsibility to their locality. This seems to me to be because so many of their members are new Christians and see less division between themselves and their neighbours than people who have been Christians all their lives and have no friends who are not Christians. They meet in converted warehouses in the heart of Liverpool, Manchester or Sheffield, to name a few I have visited, and they are where the people are.

Some of the 'gathered churches' like Steve Gaukroger's old church in Luton, find no difficulty. Others find it less natural to see themselves as part of the local community, just as some Anglican churches find themselves in leafy suburbs, where it is not so natural to speak to your neighbour anyhow! We should simply recognise that we do not necessarily come to the question with open minds.

There can be, as I have argued above, no question of the duty of the Christian church to our neighbours. We are told to love them as ourselves, to be seen like a light in a dark place, to be salt which curbs the corruption of society – and you cannot do that without being a part of the neighbourhood.

So how does the church fit into the neighbourhood in our secular, multifaith society? The very first rule is to be neighbourly. A church should be a friendly place in an unfriendly world. It should be accessible and look accessible. It should have some part of its premises to which people can drop in. A town church might have a friendly cafe; a village church its flower festivals and other occasions when people who are not members can come along on equal terms. It should, if at all possible, have members around who can chat when the church is open. It should have lunches for senior citizens; mothers and toddlers groups for young mothers; a holiday club for the children in half-term weeks and for a week in the summer. In these and in every other way it can think of, it should be a part of the local scene; a natural place for people to get together.

It is especially important for the church to be friendly when it meets together for worship on Sundays. We have developed the habit in most churches of saying hello to those around us early on in the service, so that no stranger feels neglected. And afterwards most churchgoers now stay on over a cup of coffee and ask visitors to do the same. Older members of the church make it their job to look for strange faces and welcome them. It's not just what is said from the pulpit that matters, though it matters a lot; it is the whole atmosphere of the church. It should show a group of people who do not just sing hymns about love, but who quite evidently love each other and get on well together. This matters not only for complete strangers who may look in; it matters to those who wonder what their friends would think if they brought them along.

The world today is a lonely place. In October 1996, research based on a survey by NOP reported on the misery of some of the ten million people in Britain who live alone, of whom three-quarters are under thirty-five. Many spend their time alone in a room, with only a TV for company. It reported a greater tendency for those living alone to suffer from the effects of heavy drinking and depression. Since 1970 the rate of suicide for single males has gone up by 60 per cent.

The church exists for the worship of God and for the teaching of Christians and the preaching of the gospel. But it is inherent in the command that Christians should love each other that, in the course of that, it should have an active social life. House groups enable people to spend time together; there are clubs for teenagers and young singles; young mothers get together to support each other in their new experience; and couples baby-sit for each other. Young women want advice from older women and young men from older men. Most good churches cannot help but have a vigorous social life and this, too, draws in those who are not Christians, but are lonely.

But beyond all that happens naturally, the church has a duty to organise itself to help those who are in need. It is this work, which I have described at the beginning of the book, which goes out to find those who need help and puts resources of time and money into giving the love and care of the church. It has been the work of the church down the centuries, but today it cannot be done casually. The meeting of specialised needs has to be well organised. For the same reason, no one church can meet every need, so churches in a city or district need a network, so that every need can be met and everyone knows who does what.

Of all the gifts which God gives to Christians, love is the greatest. It is love which melts the hate with which people find themselves consumed, and love which keeps society from flying apart. In the inner cities, it is love which reaches the unwanted generation who have been brought up in an atmosphere of hate. It does not matter that we are a multifaith society, or that secularism has removed people's faith in God; true unselfish love can still do its healing work.

Chapter Twelve

CHURCH AND STATE
– WHO DOES WHAT?

*Things have come to a pretty pass when religion is allowed
to interfere in the sphere of private life*

Lord Melbourne

Official religion

For the last of the British prime ministers with roots in the
eighteenth century, there was no doubt about the role of the
church. It was a part of the Establishment, but one which knew
its place. The prime minister appointed the bishops and the squire
appointed the parson, and neither bishop nor parson were expected
to enquire too closely into the affairs – public or private – of those
who appointed them.

Times have changed, but the problems of relations between
state and church are still with us. Margaret Thatcher was not
too happy with Archbishop Runcie's views on her triumphalism
after the Falklands victory or with his views on the morality of
weapons of mass destruction. And the parson today has as little
effect on the behaviour of the rich members of his parish as he
did in the eighteenth century.

Formally the Church of England is still Erastian. This means
that the prime minister still chooses the bishops and the owner
of the advowson still has the right to appoint to the living. But

the state takes even less notice of the bishops than it did in the eighteenth century, and since there are not enough clergy to go round all the parishes, the right to appoint to a living is not as valuable as it once was.

But the main difference is that the Church of England no longer enjoys a monopoly. Religious toleration has taken away all the restrictions on the rights of Catholics and the Free Churches and the Christian community no longer speaks with one voice. More than that, for the last thirty years Christianity, however formal, has no longer been seen as the final basis of the country's moral and social values and this has made for great instability. If Christians are to help to put this right, we need to know what we should consider as the proper extent of our influence.

Adjusting to toleration – the moral majority

Across the Atlantic, first the Moral Majority and now the Christian Coalition assert that the US is, despite its secular constitution, a Christian country and that its laws should be based on Christian moral values. They have formed an active group within the Republican party and, to the horror of those who want to win elections, have had a considerable effect on its public platform.

A Republican Congressman – a colleague of mine on the European Parliament/US Congress joint delegation – was faced with a challenge by the Moral Majority in a primary election. 'They never came to me as their Congressman to put their views on abortion and try to persuade me; they just started bussing people in for the primary election. But I had more experience, so I bussed in more people and won. I'd like to know what they would have done, had they won, on all the other issues Congress has to face, such as cutting tariffs to improve world trade. They know nothing about anything except this one issue.'

I have also talked since then to a very fine Christian Senator, also a Republican, and he did not see that this was an effective way of using Christian influence. The climate of opinion in the United States was now strongly secular and there was no moral majority among the voters. There were no short cuts. Those who wanted to change the law had to work first to change the climate of public opinion.

The impact of the early church on Roman and pagan society

The relationship between church and state has been an issue for the best part of the last two thousand years. The early Christians had to risk their lives on the issue. Christ had said, 'Give to Caesar the things that are Caesar's and to God the things that are God's.' So both state and church commanded the loyalty of Christians, each in its own sphere. Pilate found Jesus innocent of the Jewish charge of rebellion against the Roman state. 'I find no fault in this man.' But when Caesar asked Christians to worship him, they could not obey and many were martyred.

Paul told the Romans, 'The powers that be are ordained of God' (Rom. 13:1). So both church and state are God's creation. Until, in the fourth century, the Roman Emperor Constantine became a Christian, the empire treated the church as a Jewish sect, on which it inflicted periodic persecution. Then, for the brief remains of the empire's power, it was the official religion, and emperors – anxious that their social order should have an agreed basis – convened the bishops in councils to try to persuade them to iron out their differences and to present a united front to the public.

Then when, a hundred years later, the Roman Empire in the West began to collapse, as the barbarian tribes poured over the frontier, the church not only converted the barbarian tribes – including the Saxon and Danish invaders of England – but was the main unifying force in the social chaos which followed. As we have seen, there was a church of England before there was a king of England.

The church becomes politically powerful – and corrupt

It took a long time before the church's power as moral adjudicator became corrupted. But, in due course, as Europe became more settled, tribal chiefs who ruled at the point of the sword became kings who needed administrators. Who else was sufficiently educated and could speak Latin – still the common language of Europe – well enough to conduct difficult negotiations? So church and state became intertwined; the church became politically powerful, as mentioned above; and princes of the state, like the twelfth-century Thomas à Becket, became princes of the church. When there were disputes, as between Becket and King Henry II, appeals were made to the Bishop of Rome and the papacy became a political power in its own right.

It was the spirit of Antichrist; the incestuous relationship between church and state foretold in the book of Revelation to the apostle John. The church used its spiritual power to give authority to the state and the state, in turn, supported the church by persecuting its enemies and by making it rich. The descendants of the self-sacrificing monks who set up communities in the middle of the pagan tribes became rich with lands. Rulers who wanted to secure their place in heaven paid for the erection of the great cathedrals which sprang up to take the place of the wooden churches of the first millennium.

The other spectacular outcome of this incestuous relationship was the crusades. Instead of dealing in a spirit of love with the Saracens – as it had dealt with the Franks, the Lombards and the Saxons – the church set out to fight them with all the military might it could muster. It left a scar on the name of Christ which has survived in the Muslim world to this day and provoked a response in kind which swept away the Christian church in Asia Minor, lost Constantinople and the Balkans and brought the Turks to the gates of Vienna. As Jesus said, 'He who takes the sword will perish with the sword.'

The Reformation keeps a connection of state to church

The gospel was skewed to meet the state/church relationship and to justify the simony which sold the free grace of God for money. In England the first considered response came in the fourteenth century from an Oxford scholar, John Wyclif, who was the first to translate the Bible into English, so that the errors of the church could be plainly seen. He was also the first to set out the doctrines of the Reformation. Wyclif left behind followers in England, known as Lollards. Of more lasting importance, Wyclif was the inspiration of the first continental reformer, John Hus of Bohemia, who though martyred kept the flame alive until it was taken up by Martin Luther of Saxony, who set the whole continent alight at the beginning of the sixteenth century.

The Reformation stopped the worst abuses of the church/state relationship, but did not abandon the connection completely. There was a deeply imbued feeling that the authority of the state must have an agreed moral basis and that meant an agreed religion. The reformation settlement in Germany was that the people should follow the religion of their prince: *cuius regio eius religio*. In Switzerland, each canton chose its own religion, Protestant or Catholic. But this provoked religious wars, with the Hugenots in France fighting for religious liberty, as were the Calvinists in the Netherlands and Scotland, and the Puritans in England.

The secular state

The Puritans who emigrated to America left a legacy of opposition to state religion. The eighteenth-century constitution of the United States, though Christian in inspiration and content, was secular in presentation. Shortly afterwards the French, inspired by the American Revolution, overthrew their monarchy and proclaimed a secular state. The Russian Revolution of 1917 went even further and proclaimed an atheist state.

Most of Western Europe still retains some link between the state and the Christian faith, but in almost all countries, it is a formality. The ruling ideology in Western Europe, as in America, is a mixture of optimistic modernism and pessimistic post-modernism. The modern dogma is that there is no dogma; here is a disbelief in absolute truth of any kind. It is not only, as we have said earlier, illogical as a view; it is also absurd to ignore two thousand years of history or the size of the Christian church, however reduced, in comparison with any other religion. It is a view so corrosive – not only of moral but also of social order – that it is not sustainable. The question is not whether it will fade away, but whether it can be removed without a damaging backlash. To make sure of that, Christians need to have a well-thought-out alternative which meets the needs of British society.

Biblical teaching on church and state

1 Separation of church and state

First, it seems to me to be clear that the teaching of both Old and New Testaments is that there must be a separation of church and state. When Christ was asked why he condemned divorce, while the law of Moses had allowed for it, he said that Moses had allowed divorce, 'for the hardness of your hearts, but from the beginning it was not so'. That must mean that the civil law had to take into account the actual behaviour of the people for whom the legislation was drawn up. If people were going to divorce regardless of the moral law, then it had to be regularised in order to protect the civil status of the woman who was divorced. But that did not make divorce right; and the moral law, embodied in the ten commandments, still stood. No one was allowed to put apart what God had joined ('save for adultery' where the guilty party had already torn apart the 'one flesh').

So the church, like the Old Testament priests and prophets, must stand fast on eternal truth. It is for the state to make laws which will be obeyed even by people whose hearts and consciences are hard. A law which cannot be enforced because it does not carry broad public support is a bad law, as the Puritans found under Cromwell and as the US found in the period when the sale of alcohol was prohibited.

That does not condone totally permissive legislation. The state is ordained of God to punish wickedness and to encourage what is good. There must be a strong moral content in all legislation; but it must also be enforceable. It is for the church, like the prophets of old, to make the moral case as powerfully as it can.

2 Different disciplines

Second, the state 'does not bear the sword for nothing'. It is responsible for secular penalties. The church has a right only to warn, reprove, rebuke and exhort as the prophets did and, if members disgrace the church by their behaviour, the church should excommunicate them as a signal to the world that that kind of behaviour is not tolerable from anyone professing to be a Christian.

Paul teaches that Christians should, however, settle disputes among themselves and should not bring the church into disrepute by going to law with one another in the public courts. But if Christians are to do this, then the church has to be prepared to adjudicate, so long as there are witnesses prepared to give evidence, no matter how senior the position of the person accused of being at fault. And the judicial role of the church must be as transparent and defensible as the role of the courts. Justice must not only be done, it must be seen to be done. Where the church fails to put its own house in order and those with a complaint feel that they have to go to the public courts for justice, then great damage will be done to the church's reputation.

3 Different officers

Third, the officers of the state and church must be different. There should never again be prince-bishops capable of inflicting civil penalties on those who oppose their spiritual rule. Nor can I see how officers of the state should have the great offices of the church in their gift or that local magistrates should have the right to appoint to local church office. Both powers have almost faded out in England and it would be better were they to disappear altogether.

There is, however, nothing to prevent a Christian serving as a magistrate or in any other public office, so long as they do not run for office *as Christians*. I was responsible for the leading negotiations for my political group when we wanted to join the predominantly Christian Democratic group in the European Parliament. I said that in Britain no party ran for office claiming to be the 'Christian' party, since all parties contained Christians and we felt that no one could claim to be more Christian than any other nor use their faith to get elected. I was supported by one of our Jewish members, which helped to make the point, and our argument was accepted with only the Dutch Christian Democrat opposing.

The Christian church claims to teach truth as it has been revealed by God. Ordained ministers have to be sure that they do not mix their own personal political judgment, which is fallible, with the word of God which carries divine authority. I was once at a dinner where Peter Walker, then an MP, complained to a politically minded bishop that it was all very well for him to pontificate from the pulpit on the need for more houses, but he did not have the rough job of deciding who would go without so that the extra houses could be paid for.

'Politics is the art of the possible'

Politics is not about absolute truth; it is about what is best in the circumstances. Views on that will differ, depending on our different experience and backgrounds and, with elected politicians, depending on what are the needs of those who elected them. Politicians may be mistaken; and if they are, it is better to have them change their minds than to make them feel that they have to stick obstinately to some old view through thick and thin.

Many Christians may still worry that, if they were elected politicians, party politics would force them to approve policies with which they do not agree and that that would be morally wrong. Most parties have a 'conscience clause', under which MPs can vote against the whip, if they feel that their basic beliefs really cannot be reconciled with the party line. On more mundane matters, politicians cannot be experts on everything which comes before them, and the political process would be impossible unless they were prepared to trust their party colleagues to hammer out a party position on issues on which they were more competent. And on issues on which we are knowledgeable and competent, we still have to find a line on which everyone can agree. There is no dishonour in conceding points to others as we would want them to concede on another occasion to us. As that great politician, Rab Butler, once said, 'Politics is the art of the possible'.

If there is a difference between the Christian and their colleagues, it might be that the Christian will sit looser to politics than those for whom politics, and success at politics, is the whole of their life. It is, as I was told by my first constituency chairman, 'a rough old trade' and we have to be prepared for ups and downs, for doing what we can in an imperfect world and not taking it too tragically if everything does not go our way. But we will have moments when we know that it was for that occasion, if for nothing else, that we were called to be a politician and to stand fast on what we believe.

4 The state's duty of tolerance

Fourth, the state has a duty to ensure that there is toleration for all religions. We cannot press other states to allow toleration for Christians if we are not prepared to tolerate their religions in our own country.

There was indignation among Christians when a mosque was built in Regent's Park, London. Since my company was building it, I thought I should find out just how it came to be built there and was told that the land was given in exchange for land for a Christian church in Cairo. Much later I was helped by the Egyptian representative when I asked, successfully, for religious liberty to be placed on the agenda of the Euro-Arab dialogue.

I was once asked to go to Ankara to argue the case for protection against police harassment of the tiny Protestant churches. I was able to base their case on the Turkish constitution, which guaranteed them freedom of worship. The Turkish government was extremely helpful and gave the practical protection needed.

In our present culture, where anything goes, there is still much anxiety about the limits of toleration. This worry is especially apparent in Eastern Europe, where they are having to make up their minds on the limits, if any, to their new freedom. I met officials of the Ministry of Cults of a newly independent Eastern European state two years ago. I was anxious that they should not treat the mainstream Protestant churches as sects. I found them worried that an army of footloose Americans had arrived in their country with a great deal of money and literature, and they did not know whether they were from genuine churches or from way-out sects.

I told them that the European Parliament had given the problem of sects a lot of attention a few years ago and came to the conclusion that the law of most countries was enough to deal with antisocial activity, and that no sect or religion was above the law. In the meantime, I said, if their ideas were mad, most people would see through them. At which the main official leant over and said, 'But we want to make sure that our people see that they are mad!'

Christians should be in favour of religious toleration. Christian churches need the protection of laws on toleration in China and in all those countries which have one predominant and non-Christian religion: Muslim in Turkey, Egypt, Indonesia, Iraq, Pakistan and Indonesia; Hindu in India; and Buddhist in Thailand. In the open market of ideas, the Christian faith has flourished more than any other. So we have nothing to fear from tolerance and everything to gain; and we should be content that our moral order and the social order arising from it can be put forward and defended on their merits.

At present we have less to fear from other religions in Britain than we have from secular humanism. The other faiths are far more in agreement with the Christians than they are with the humanists. They agree with a moral order, giving high priority to the family, and a social order depending on it. They are as opposed as we are to the deconstruction popular among humanists; the dogma that there can be no dogma; the relativism which abolishes right and wrong, where sentimentality smothers justice.

5 The prophetic ministry of the church

Fifth, the church has a prophetic ministry to which the state is bound to listen and which it ignores at its peril. It is the duty of the state to keep as close to the moral law as possible, for a state which does not encourage the keeping of moral law is doomed to disaster.

The apostle Paul told the Romans that the state was ordained by God to punish evil and encourage good. If it does not fulfil these moral functions, it abandons its divine authority. The Old Testament prophets attack the state for its carelessness about justice; its failure to look after those who cannot look after themselves: the poor, the fatherless, the widows and the aliens. They condemn rulers who take bribes and pervert justice and who encourage the people to follow false gods.

These judgments are not just addressed to God's own people. They are addressed to all the nations round about, to the Assyrians, Babylonians, Egyptians, Edomites, Moabites, Ammonites and Philistines. At one point the Assyrians repent and judgment is suspended. But in the end Nineveh is condemned to disappear for ever, as is Babylon. On the other hand, Egypt is to remain, but never again to be a powerful nation. Damascus remains to this day, as does the Ammonite capital, now Amman. Hostility to their neighbours is high on the list of their sins. So a state should try to live at peace with its neighbours and not threaten them; to respect and help them and not oppress them.

Just as God has given a conscience to every individual, so he expects nations, too, to know what is right and wrong, even if they do not have the benefit of the written law. And it is by their obedience to this law in their collective conscience that they will be judged.

Abraham prayed to God that, for the sake of ten righteous people in Sodom and Gomorrah, God would spare the cities. God agreed, but there were not ten righteous ones and the cities were destroyed.

For it is clear that God not only judges individuals, he also judges nations. So the church, in its prophetic role, is entitled to stimulate and articulate the conscience of the state; to make sure that those who are overlooked, who have no political clout, receive natural justice. If false prophets say that there is no absolute right and wrong, the church is bound to point out that there is and that without a clear recognition of right and wrong there will be no justice. If rulers and people worship the false idols of power, money and sex, then the church has to say clearly and plainly that they are false idols; that they lead people astray; and that the state should see them for what they are and do what it can to discourage their worship.

We are taught that the Christian church is the salt of the earth, to save it from corruption. But Christ also warned of a salt that had lost its savour, which was fit only to be thrown out. So an inactive church, a church which does not use its prophetic gift and warn its neighbours that God judges nations, will save neither itself nor its nation.

6 The state is temporal and the church is eternal

Sixth, the state is temporal and can fail; the church is eternal and will not fail. Christians are to be in the world, but not of it. Daniel is perhaps the best prototype. He was a very senior official in the Babylonian Empire, but he and his three Jewish companions made it quite clear from the beginning that they held to their own moral code. As young Jewish exiles on probation, they kept to their own strict dietary rules and later, as senior officials at the emperor's court, they would not worship his statue. They were rulers of the doomed empire, but clearly apart from it. Daniel was not at Belshazzar's feast. When the writing appeared on the wall, he had to be sent for.

When Babylon was taken by the Medes and Persians, they knew that Daniel was not a part of Babylonian society and they also engaged him as administrator of their empire. This caused great jealousy among the chief officers of the new empire. They tried to exclude him by making his form of worship illegal, but he continued, at the risk of his life, and God protected him.

So there may come a time when the politics of our ruling party or our country become so corrupt that no Christian should be identified with them. Christians in Central and Eastern Europe felt that they could not become members of the Communist party, because of its explicit atheism. So they were excluded from universities and all public service; and, now that communism has gone, the church is vindicated. But in Germany a great many Christians became Nazi party members, to the great damage of the German church.

If a party is overtaken by racialist and nationalist prejudice or rides with the spirit of greed instead of resisting it, then Christians have to remove themselves lest they too be identified with these prejudices. But if there is still, in the party, a group which stands by its principles and is big enough to fight back, then a Christian should think twice before quitting the battle.

No one wants to go into exile but there were Puritans in the seventeenth century who felt that the struggle was lost and left for New England. Yet there were also Puritans who felt that they had to stay behind to defend the Reformation settlement and, despite the temporary restoration of the Stuart kings, the Reformation settlement survived. All across the south of Scotland there are monuments to the deaths of the Covenanters who stayed where they were and refused to give up their faith. If it ever comes to that in Britain, we will need a faith as stout as theirs.

The church's secret weapon

The Christian church has exercised a powerful influence for over two thousand years in every kind of society and culture. But its weapons have not been the weapons of this world. The secret weapon of the Christian church is not to be found in any military arsenal or in any party manifesto. It is, very simply, the love of Christ.

Paul tells us that of all the gifts, the greatest is love. The heart of the Christian message is that God the Son so loved the world that he came to earth to suffer all the human hazards and hurt; and above all to suffer the consequences of God's justice so that we might be saved from its condemnation ourselves. There is no greater love than that a person should lay down their life for their friend. But Christ died for those who were his enemies, so that they could become his friends and, more than that, become part of his family. In return he demands the same love from his followers. 'Love your enemies, do good to those who hate you, pray for those who despitefully use you.'

He is the example for all Christians. He not only taught the people; he cared for them. When, after the sermon, his disciples wanted to send the people away, he said that they had had nothing to eat and would collapse on the way; they had to have something to eat before they started home. People, he taught, do not live by bread alone; but bread was also necessary. He healed people because he loved them. He had created man and woman perfect and their sickness was a sign of what they had lost which he could and should restore. So the paralytic took up his bed and walked; the lame leapt; the lepers' skin was made pure; the fever vanished; the deaf heard; the dumb spoke and the blind saw. He himself not only healed but he also gave the gift of healing to the apostles. The care of the body as well as the soul became part of their ministry. James said in his epistle, 'Faith without works is useless' (James 2:20).

Love for the needs of others was a sign of true faith and its absence raised doubts as to whether a profession of faith was really true: 'Suppose a brother or sister is without clothes and daily food. If one of you says to him, "Keep warm and well fed" but does nothing about his physical needs, what good is it?' (James 2:15, 16). We are saved by faith in Christ's death and not by works, but if nothing changes in our lives it shows that nothing has changed in our hearts. As Paul said at his trial, 'I preached that they should repent and turn to God and prove their repentance by their deeds' (Acts 26:20).

Perhaps the most vivid illustration of Christian love is the account by Luke of Paul's voyage which ended in shipwreck on Malta. Paul had some of the grimmest companions on that last recorded journey. The passengers were criminals; the soldiers guarding them wanted to kill them all before they could get to shore; and the sailors tried to make off in the longboat and leave the rest to drown. Paul might well have decided that he had fought the good fight and that, if God now wanted to call him home, he would be content. Instead we find him full of care about the safety of his fellow-travellers. He came from those coasts and knew the winds and weather. He warned that, since they had been delayed, it was now too late in the year to sail from Crete. But the Roman commander listened to the impatient captain.

Then came the storm of which Paul had warned, and the ship was driven before it day and night until the captain and crew despaired. But Paul had been praying for them and told them that God had assured him that though the ship would be wrecked, they would all be saved. So they stayed at their posts, and soon the soundings showed that they were near land. Paul, ever on the alert, found that the crew were going to use the longboat to leave the ship and abandon the others to their fate. He told the Roman centurion, who made the soldiers cut off the boat. Then Paul said that unless they all had a meal, they would be too weak to get to shore, so they ate. All of them made it from the sandbank through the breakers to the shore. And our final picture is of the great evangelist gathering sticks for a fire to dry them all out!

It was that spirit of Christian love for those around them which converted the pagan Roman world and created the church which survived the decadent Roman Empire. We know not only from historians but also from the first chapters of Paul's own letter to the Romans about the decadence of pagan culture. However bad things are today, they are no worse than those which faced the early Christians. The rising paganism of Britain is nothing to the firmly established paganism of Rome. The humanism of Britain today is weak compared with the powerful schools of Greek philosophy. And we do not face active persecution and death for failure to worship a false god.

But despite all that, during the first century people turned to the Christian faith in increasing numbers. In an age when there was no mass communication, it can only have come about by the example of Christian neighbours and by the reasons they gave for their faith. Slaves suddenly gave better service; no longer answered back, no longer pilfered, no longer slacked on the job. Neighbours showed love and care to those in need; their children were better behaved. People they had known all their lives and who were no better than they should be were suddenly transformed; easier to live with, kinder, more thoughtful and helpful, prepared to sit and listen, more forgiving and much happier than they had ever been.

Peter told the church to be 'prepared to give an answer to everyone who asks you a reason for the faith that is in you'. Their neighbours, whom they had known all their lives, would come to ask them, so they had to know what to say. That was why, though there were official persecutions, it seemed to the people themselves odd that the empire was condemning its best citizens to death. So persecutions were not usually widespread and seldom sustained for long.

Not much more than a century later, the pagan tribes from the north were sweeping over the Rhine and through the Alpine passes, overrunning the churches in Gaul, Lombardy and Britain and then streaming south into Spain and to Rome itself. Roman citizens felt that the end had come. But the church sent out missionaries to these tribes, established simple communities among them and converted them. That was the pattern of the Roman mission to Canterbury, of the Celtic mission from Ireland to Iona in Scotland and of the onward mission first to Lindisfarne and then to all northern England. It was also the pattern of the mission of an Englishman, Wynfrith, better known as Boniface, to central Germany.

What was clear of these missionaries, above all, is that they came in love. Though they had to have the permission of the rulers, they established themselves in the hearts of the common people by living among them in rough communities and caring for them.

It is incredible, humanly speaking, that the terrifying invaders – the Visigoths and Vandals, the Lombards and Franks, the Saxons and later the Vikings, strong enough to break the greatest empire in the world – were converted by love and put away their age-old pagan gods so quietly. There was no longer a disciplined Roman state and no superior political power left to put down the quarrels of the petty rulers as they fought each other to establish their claims to the new lands. But there was a broadly accepted moral law, which gave birth to a social system. This grew until from chaos emerged a new rule of law.

In looking back to pre-Reformation Europe, Protestants are apt only to see the church as it was at the Reformation, with the accumulated corruptions of the previous three or four centuries, and to ignore the remarkable history of the first millennium. This is partly because, except for the brief period between Constantine and the dark ages, so much is unrecorded. It is also because the medieval church claimed that all the practices to which the Protestants objected at the Reformation were based on precedents which went back to the beginning of the church's history. The Reformers themselves did not take that view. Calvin based much of his interpretation on the great Augustine, late fourth-century/early fifth-century Bishop of Hippo, rather than on the customs which had become established since his day.

As we have seen earlier, the love of Christians for their neighbours and the care of the church for those who were in need have gone together in the great revivals of the faith in every century from the Reformation until the nineteenth century. But, a hundred years ago, Christians in Britain began to look towards their own needs rather than those of their neighbours and there has been no great revival to compare with those which went before.

I looked through the hymn-book of a church where I was due to preach on the Good Samaritan and found it almost impossible to find a suitable hymn. It is right, of course, that hymns should be focused on our relationship with God. We are in church to worship. But these hymns seemed to my searching eye to have more to do with us and our subjective feelings than with the great God whom we worship. And I found it incredible that there should be nothing on our love for our neighbours in need.

An inward-looking church

We seem, for the last hundred years, to have become a church more in search of the 'feel-good factor'. There is a lot of talk of experiences to make us holy. But there is no quick fix for holiness. It comes slowly as we learn to grow in love for God and, as that love dictates, to fulfil our duty and to back faith with deeds. It is not something we ever attain completely in this life. Those who seem most holy are those who are most aware of their faults. The apostle Paul wrote of himself as the 'chief of sinners'.

Our care for our neighbour has been subliminated in mass evangelism. If people will not come to church, maybe they can be persuaded to go to expensively advertised rallies with charismatic speakers and a massed choir. But though some people do become Christians at mass rallies, these are not a reflection of the great spontaneous upsurge which marked the classic revivals of the past.

The new liberal wing of the Protestant churches followed the German fashion of 'higher criticism', which removed the authority of the texts on which Protestant teaching was based. They took over the leadership in social care from the evangelicals. The liberals filled the gap left by their reluctance to preach the gospel of sin and salvation by preaching the 'social gospel'. As mentioned above, this taught that the kingdom of God was to be achieved on earth by social action. To the evangelicals this sounded like salvation by works and, as such, they quite rightly denounced it. This identification of social action with liberal theology made it difficult, decades later, to persuade evangelicals that care for our neighbours was in the mainstream of Christian doctrine and of Reformed, Puritan, Methodist and evangelical tradition.

The liberal repudiation of the mainstream Christian beliefs emptied their churches. People did not see the need to go to sit on a hard pew when they could sit in their own comfortable armchairs and read the same views in the Sunday newspapers. So the resources of the churches dried up and the social gospel became an exhortation from the pulpit to the politicians. But politicians are very alert to the capacity of people who address them to deliver corresponding public support and, as church attendance decreased, so did the political influence of the church.

Evangelicals recover their tradition of social concern

The good news is that in the last thirty years, as the moral order has been crumbling and the social problems rising, there has been a renewed concern among the evangelical wing of the church for the needs of our neighbours. The sheer volume of distress had made an impact on the churches. As the social services fail to cope with the overload, an increasing number of people and their problems come to the church door, as they used to do before the welfare state.

As we have mentioned the Churches of England and Scotland, with their parish system, have always felt a need for all those in the parish, whether they come to church or not. So it is more natural for them to get back into their stride in looking after the needs around them. But, too often, their churches and resources are not in the right places. The Church Urban Fund was set up to help to deal with that problem and though it is doing a good job, the size of the problem has leapt far ahead of the new resources.

Travelling round the country I have found that those churches which are heavy with new converts see no reason why their neighbours should not find the same Christian faith that they have found. For that reason they are nearer to the needs of their neighbours. The churches which have most difficulty are those with a membership which consists of long-committed Christians, who are less likely to socialise with those who are not Christians and more likely to be cut off from the needs around them.

Christians who take their secular calling seriously – who work hard and save their money – are likely to have moved out to the more affluent suburbs. For instance, the city-centre church in which I attended Sunday school, with boys from working-class families in the streets around, has now moved out to a far better district beside the university campus. These, however, are the churches with the talents and annual budgets of up to £100,000.

There is also a group whose doctrine of the sovereignty of God seems to inhibit them from active concern for those outside the church. They see clearly the limitations of mass evangelism. They look to God to send again the great revivals of the past in which the Holy Spirit roused a sense of sin and need which is quite beyond the ability of any human agency. So they preach the truth and pray for revival but seem immune, meanwhile, to the desperate plight of those immediately around them or to the plain command to Christians to love their neighbour in the very practical way in which Christ and the early church loved those who lived beside them.

I once spoke to the aging membership of a city mission where they told me that the truth was preached every Sunday for everyone who wanted to come. But when I asked how many from round about actually came, it was clear that the preaching was entirely to the faithful. Not far away there was a community church meeting in a former warehouse where, no doubt, the doctrine was not so deep; but it was clear that it was the centre for the whole neighbourhood and not just for the faithful.

Christian action networks

Patchily, hesitantly and as yet inadequately, the churches are attempting to do more in each of our cities to deal with the desperate needs – as we have seen in Chapter 2.

There now seems to be broad agreement in many cities that their church-based projects should form a network so that everyone knows who does what and a church knows where to send those who come to their door in need of help. The first group of churches to have this idea was in the city of Worcester, not the sort of place one might have thought had a lot of problems. But beyond the cathedral close were all the problems we had come across elsewhere.

The Evangelical Alliance is trying to develop a national link between city networks, so that we pass on good ideas between people in the same kind of work, make sure they know about national expertise, help in fund-raising and have a better dialogue with the social services.

Projects such as drug rehabilitation need a lot of technical expertise and a link to a national body to guide and supervise that part of their work. Not all projects have access to the best national expertise and we hope that we can make those connections. The rising tide of misery and need is plunging the churches into work in which they have had little recent experience and so everyone is busy reinventing the wheel all on their own. We need a structure which helps us to learn from each other as fast as possible. In every city we visit we find projects which seem to have solved problems with which others are still grappling, and we need to make those role models known as widely and as quickly as we can.

Within a dozen cities so far, churches are setting up for each of their networks a lay leadership team whose job is to keep their city's needs in front of their churches, to tap the reservoir of lay talent needed to man the projects and to keep the churches' work and concerns in front of the city.

These networks are very new and still feeling their way. We have found that it is not enough for the enthusiasts running the projects to get together; they need the interest and weight of the churches behind them with the whole-hearted support of the church leaders. Where the churches have swung behind the idea, it has gone ahead; and where they have not yet got agreement, it has held fire.

Before they commit themselves, the church leaders have to be persuaded that this is not another set of meetings and paperwork on an overburdened minister. It is a job for the men and women in the pew who have experience in the practical problems with which the projects have to deal. There are, in one church or another, those with practical experience in the social services, in medicine, in teaching, in the police and in all the other professions which can be helpful to the projects in the network.

So, where networks have been set up, there is a group of such people responsible for helping them and for assuring the churches that the projects to which they have given their support are being run to the best professional standards and within the regulations which today, quite rightly, protect the public against abuse. They will also, we hope, help to find volunteers and the funding – public or private – on which all voluntary projects depend.

The Evangelical Alliance has the advantage that it can put together a network across a membership which spans all the Protestant denominations and those few which are not members, but also hold a similar basis of faith. The consensus among those who have set up networks is that while it is necessary to have this kind of widely spread and theologically grounded sponsorship to set up local networks and to run them, we have to work with all the existing efforts, such as the Church of Scotland's Board of Social Responsibility, and the similar Board for the Presbyterian Church in Ireland, and the diocesan organisations in England, all of which have been very helpful. It is my impression that a great deal of their work is, as one would expect, in meeting long-standing needs, while we are trying mainly to deal with the needs which have arisen from the moral and social collapse of the last thirty years.

When we visited Worcester, they decided to use the occasion to make a public launch and packed the largest church in the city, inviting local radio and press to attend. The radio interview was very sympathetic and the *Worcester Journal* gave us the front page with the banner headline, 'FROM PULPIT TO PAVEMENT'. People know the needs around them and welcome the idea that the churches are there to help. So we have asked the new networks – when they think that they are all set up and ready to answer questions – to have a public launch and to ask along the local media and also the local councillors, social services and MPs. Then not only will the churches know where to send people in need, but so will everyone else.

However much the House of Commons may be attached to humanism as a guiding light, members know all too well the awful problems in their own constituencies. I met a senior Cabinet minister at a dinner, talked about the problems in his own city and about the network we were just about to set up. He has a reputation for a tough, no-nonsense, attitude; but on this he was with me all the way, especially reassured when I told him that the black churches were also included and that the network had a black leader .

The strength of the humanists is in the national media. But they are not on the ground as we are and our democracy, with all its faults, is based on people who live in some councillor's ward, some MP's constituency. That is the ultimate source of power in a democracy. When I was an MEP for Cambridgeshire, it was those half million voters who mattered. Circulars with a London postmark went into the bin; but every letter with a local address was answered, every problem dealt with. The *Cambridge Evening News* and the *Peterborough Evening Telegraph* were the papers which mattered. My office and assistant were in the Shire Hall, Cambridge; the people to whom I listened were the members of my constituency council, mostly county and district councillors. That is where the church needs to make its efforts if we are to be heard.

Christians believe that the greatest need of men and women is to be reconciled to our Creator through the work of Jesus Christ on the cross and to have eternal life. But that is not an easy message to give to a secular world which does not believe in a Creator or in eternal life. To look after our neighbours is not only right and Christian; it is the way in which we earn our right to be heard. I once opened a new church on a tough housing estate in Cambridge. It was the mayor's own ward and before the service began, he said, 'I don't know what these people teach, but I know what they do for our children and our old folk, so I have come along to listen.'

The early church were people who 'turned the world upside down', and if we want to have the same impact, we will do it in the same way by caring for our neighbours in need.

CONCLUSION

Put not your trust in princes. (Psa. 146:3)

Princes or our rulers of today cannot be relied on, because they are subject to so many conflicting pressures. Someone asked Harold Macmillan what he found was his chief problem as prime minister. He said, 'Events.' It is only too easy for government to be blown off course by events which no one could have foreseen. Sometimes it is even happy to be blown off course, so that it can have an excuse for what it has failed to do. So though we may map a course for government, we would be unwise to rely on it.

It is possible that a new government will do all that we ask of it. It may raise taxes so that we have lower interest rates and higher investment and that, gradually, we will start on the road back to full employment. It may even join monetary union in the first wave, and we may have even lower and much more competitive interest rates and investment, and the growth of the number of jobs may go much faster.

It is also possible that a new government will reform the constitution so that it is impossible for an autocratic party to get into power on a minority vote. It may, if we are fortunate, put other needed safeguards in the constitution, which will make democracy and freedom of speech much more secure. It may even take a lead in Europe and insist that our partners in the union go with us in an effort to get the whole European economy moving in a way which would soak up employment in a much shorter time.

Or maybe none of these things will happen. In that case the

217

outlook is bleak. So everyone who believes in the power of prayer should pray for wisdom and vision for our rulers. And everyone who has a political lever, even if it is only asking questions at a local meeting (not so difficult because they are so badly attended), should brief themselves, and maybe the local press too, and go along and do their bit.

There is, unfortunately, another all too plausible scenario. The new government fails to do anything to deal with the problems of the internal and external deficit or of unemployment. Its revenues are therefore not sufficiently buoyant to do what is needed for the public sector, and the increasing demands for education, health, pensions and social security are not met. So the public loses confidence. The rate of crime goes on rising; the police are no longer able to guarantee public safety; and private volunteers take their place, a good deal less careful about the treatment they give to those who get in their way.

Behind these private armies rises a political organisation, which soon has control of the streets in the inner cities. And, at the back of that political group rises a populist party, dedicated to the restoration of law and order, to the removal of Britain from the 'shackles' of Europe and to the restoration of all the old values.

It gains all the anti-European votes. It is backed by the tabloids and it begins to negotiate with the nationalist section of the divided and dispirited opposition. The final voting alliance is seen by that section of the opposition as the best way of getting back into power and it gives an aura of respectability to the newcomers. The populist party gets the votes of the 20 per cent who are out of work or in sweated labour. The nationalist wing of the opposition brings their combined vote in the next election to 39 per cent – just enough to give them a bare majority of seats – and their leader becomes prime minister.

He takes office with a mandate to restore order, declares that he cannot do this without special powers, and these are voted through the Commons without any other constitutional check to stop them. That is the end of freedom of speech and of British democracy.

Maybe there is only a five to one chance of this happening. But that is near enough to take no risks. I believe that we should all do our best to see that it does not happen. Secular humanism would not survive, but the Christian church would come through, as the German church survived the Nazis and the Russian church survived the Communists. But it would be a terrible time.

So we should do our best as Christians to see that it never happens. We should, of course, pray. But those who ask God to act are obliged, in all conscience, to do what they can to bring about whatever it is that they pray for. So we should do what we can by becoming much more active citizens than we have been until now.

But we should also put all our hearts and souls into the awful problems faced by our neighbours: women bringing up children all alone; children not wanted by parents; and those incapable of finding training and a job without our help. We should ensure that the big estates in our cities are no longer no-go areas for Christians.

Our ministers should preach the need to love our neighbours; and our lay leaders should organise ways in which we can help them, either on our own or in a network of churches working together. Rich churches should help poor inner-city churches with money, and churches with lots of talent should offer help to those who have less.

As I have looked back over our history, I have been struck by the way in which care for society has gone hand in hand with revival. How can we pray for God's blessing on our land if we are not willing to do what we can to help? How can people believe in the love of God when we – who are supposed to be the temple of the Holy Spirit, God's outward evidence on earth – do not show our love in a way that they would understand? Is it any wonder that the care for 'the relief of man's estate' went together with enormous expansion of the Christian church? Is it surprising that when we are more anxious to get blessing for ourselves than for others, we get it for neither?

I do not put my trust in princes. I put it in the power of God to work first in our own hearts to make us see our duty for our own neighbours, in the town or city where he has placed us. Then, when we do that, I believe that he will bless us with a spiritual power which we have not seen for over a hundred years. We will not receive this power by going to conventions to find a blessing for ourselves. We will receive it by going out to do our duty.